Norton Anthology of
WESTERN MUSIC

SECOND EDITION
VOLUME I

Medieval • Renaissance • Baroque

Also available from Norton

An Anthology of Early Renaissance Music
Edited by Noah Greenberg and Paul Maynard

Anthology of Medieval Music
Edited by Richard H. Hoppin

The Norton Scores: An Anthology for Listening
Fourth Edition: Standard and Expanded
Edited by Roger Kamien

The Concerto, 1800–1900
Edited by Paul Henry Lang

The Symphony, 1800–1900
Edited by Paul Henry Lang

Anthology of Romantic Music
Edited by Leon Plantinga

Choral Music: A Norton Historical Anthology
Edited by Ray Robinson

Norton Anthology of
WESTERN MUSIC

SECOND EDITION

VOLUME I

Medieval • Renaissance • Baroque

EDITED BY

CLAUDE V. PALISCA

Yale University

W • W • Norton & Company New York • London

The text of this book is composed in Times Roman,
with display type set in Bembo.
Composition by Vail-Ballou Press
of the Maple-Vail Book Group.

Second Edition

Library of Congress Cataloging in Publication Data
ISBN 0-393-95642-3 Vol. I
ISBN 0-393-95644-X Vol. II

W. W. Norton & Company, Inc., 500 Fifth Avenue, New York, N.Y. 10110
W. W. Norton & Company Ltd., 37 Great Russell Street, London WC1B 3NU

3 4 5 6 7 8 9 0

CONTENTS

SECULAR MONOPHONY

ARS ANTIQUA

Ars Nova

RENAISSANCE

Motet

Mass

CHANSON, LIED, CANTO CARNASCIALESCO

FROTTOLA AND MADRIGAL

INSTRUMENTAL

BAROQUE

ARIA, AIR, AND MADRIGAL

PREFACE

The title of this anthology lacks one important qualifier: it is an *historical* anthology of western music. There is a wide difference between an historical anthology and one intended simply to supply a selection of music for study and analysis.

Historians cannot confine themselves to studying the great works that are the usual stuff of anthologies in splendid isolation. They are interested in products of the imagination great and small as they exist in a continuum of such works. Just as composers did not create in a musical void, standing aloof from the models of their predecessors and contemporaries, so the historically-oriented student and analyst must have the primary material that permits establishing historical connections. This anthology invites students and teachers to make such connections. It confronts, for example, important works and their models, pieces written on a common subject or built according to similar procedures or that give evidence of subtle influences of one composer's work on another's.

Most music before 1500 was composed on some pre-existent music, and there are numerous examples of this practice even after that date. Whenever possible in this anthology, the music that served to ignite a composer's imagination is provided. In one notable case a single chant gave rise to a chain of polyphonic elaborations. This is the Alleluia with verse, *Alleluia Pascha nostrum* (NAWM 16), elaborated by Léonin in organum purum with clausulae, refreshed with substitute clausulae by his successors; and both his and the new clausulae were turned into motets by adapting Latin or French texts to them or made fuller with new parts both with and without texts. (This Alleluia set, although different in content, format and realization, is itself modeled on similar sets on this chant devised by Richard Crocker and Karl Kroeger as local teaching aids, and I am indebted to them for the general idea and certain details.)

A similar chain of works are the masses built upon the melisma on the word *caput* in the Sarum version of the Antiphon, *Venit ad Petrum:* two are here given, the first by Obrecht, and the second by Ockeghem, each influencing the other (NAWM 40 and 41). It is instructive similarly to observe in Josquin's early motet, *Tu solus, qui facis mirabilia* (NAWM 32), the way he absorbed fragments of Ockeghem's arrangement of the song, *D'ung aultre amer* (NAWM 48), or to be able to refer to the *Benedictus* of Taverner's Mass, *Gloria tibi trinitas* (NAWM 42), the source of the famous subject,

In nomine, when studying one of the many variations upon it, such as that by Christopher Tye (NAWM 65). The process of coloration and variation that produced Luys de Narváez's arrangement for vihuela (NAWM 49b) may be inferred from comparing it to the original polyphonic chanson *Mille regretz* by Josquin (NAWM 49a). A later example of this process, starting with a monodic model, may be found in the *Lachrimae* pavans of Dowland and Byrd (NAWM 102a and b) based on the well-known air, *Flow my tears,* by Dowland (NAWM 69). In the twentieth century the variation procedure is the structural principle for several excerpts, namely those by Strauss (NAWM 146), Schoenberg (NAWM 148), and Copland (NAWM 150). Arcadelt's parody in his Mass (NAWM 43) of Mouton's motet, *Noe, noe* (NAWM 34) may be assumed to be a tribute.

Subtler connections may be detected between Lully's overture to *Armide* (No. 75a) and the opening chorus of Bach's cantata, *Nun komm, der Heiden Heiland* (NAWM 90), between Gossec's *Marche lugubre* (NAWM 117) and the Funeral March from Beethoven's "Eroica" Symphony (NAWM 118), between the nocturnes of Field and Chopin (NAWM 125 and 126), or between Musorgsky's song *Bez solntsa* (NAWM 158) and Debussy's *Nuages* (NAWM 144).

Comparison of the musical realization of the same dramatic moments in the legend of Orpheus by Peri and Monteverdi (NAWM 71 and 72) reveal the latter's debts to the former. It is revealing to compare the settings of Mignon's song from Goethe's *Wilhelm Meister* by Schubert, Schumann, and Wolf (NAWM 133, 134, and 135).

Some of the selections betray foreign influences, as the penetration of Italian styles in England in Purcell's songs for *The Fairy Queen* (NAWM 76) or Humfrey's verse and anthem (NAWM 88). The crisis in Handel's career, brought on partly by the popularity of the ballad opera and the English audience's rejection of his own Italian *opera seria,* is documented in a scene from *The Beggar's Opera* (NAWM 81) and by the changes within his own dramatic *oeuvre* (NAWM 80, 82 and 89). The new Italian style to which he also reacted is exemplified by Pergolesi's *La serva padrona* (NAWM 121).

Some composers are represented by more than one work to permit comparison of early and late styles—Josquin, Monteverdi, Bach, Handel, Vivaldi, Haydn, Beethoven, Liszt, Schoenberg, Stravinsky—or to show diverse approaches by a single composer to distinct genres—Machaut, Dufay, Ockeghem, Arcadelt, Willaert, Monteverdi, Bach, Mozart.

A number of the pieces marked new departures in their day, for example Adrian Willaert's *Aspro core* from his *Musica nova* (NAWM 57), Viadana's solo concerto, *O Domine Jesu Christe* (NAWM 84), Rousseau's scene from *Le Devin du village* (NAWM 122), or C. P. E. Bach's sonata (NAWM 108). Other pieces were chosen particularly because they were singled out by contemporary critics, such as Arcadelt's *Ahime, dov'è 'l bel viso* (NAWM 56), hailed in 1549 by Bishop Cirillo Franco as a ray of hope for the future of text-expressive music; or Monteverdi's *Cruda Amarilli* (NAWM 67), dismembered by Artusi in his dialogue of 1600 that is at once a critique and a defense of Monteverdi's innovations; Caccini's *Perfidissimo volto* (NAWM 66), mentioned in the preface to his own *Euridice* as one of his pioneering attempts, or Cesti's *Intorno all'idol mio* (NAWM 74), one of the most cited arias of the mid-seventeenth century. Others are Lully's monologue in *Armide, Enfin il est en ma puissance* (NAWM 75b), which was roundly criticized by Rousseau and carefully analyzed by Rameau and d'Alembert; the scene of Carissimi's *Jephte* (NAWM 86), singled out by Athanasius Kircher as a triumph of the powers of musical expression; and the *Danse des adolescentes* in Stravinsky's *Le Sacre* (NAWM 147), the object of a critical uproar after its premiere.

Certain of the items serve to correct commonplace misconceptions about the history of music. Cavalieri's *Dalle più alte sfere* (NAWM 70) of 1589 shows that florid monody existed well before 1600. The movements from Clementi's and Dussek's sonatas (NAWM 109 and 110) reveal an intense romanticism and an exploitation of the piano that surpass Beethoven's writing of the same period and probably influenced it. The movement from Richter's String Quartet (NAWM 111) tends to refute Haydn's paternity of the genre. Sammartini's and Stamitz's symphonic movements (NAWM 113 and 114) show that there was more than one path to the Viennese symphony. The Allegro from Johann Christian Bach's E-flat Harpsichord Concerto (NAWM 119) testifies to Mozart's dependence (NAWM 120) on this earlier model. The scene from Meyerbeer's *Les Huguenots* (NAWM 139) is another seminal work that left a trail of imitations.

Most of the selections, however, are free of any insinuations on the part of this editor. They are simply typical, superlative creations that represent their makers, genres, or times outstandingly. Most of the *Ars nova* and many of the Renaissance works are in this category, as are a majority of those of the Baroque, Romantic, and Modern periods. My choices mark important turning points and shifts of style, historical phenomena that are interesting if not always productive of great music, new models of constructive procedures, typical moments in the work of individual composers, and always challenging exemplars for historical and structural analysis.

The proportion of space assigned to a composer or work is not a reflection of my estimation of his greatness, and, regretfully, numerous major figures could not be represented at all. In an anthology of limited size every work chosen excludes another of corresponding size that is equally worthy. Didactic functionality, historical illumination, intrinsic musical quality rather than "greatness" or "genius" were the major criteria for selection.

The inclusion of a complete Office (NAWM 4) and a nearly complete Mass (NAWM 3) deserves special comment. I realize that the rituals as represented here have little validity as historical documents of the Middle Ages. It would have been more authentic, perhaps, to present a mass and office as practiced in a particular place at a particular moment, say in the twelfth century. Since the Vatican Council, the liturgies printed here are themselves archaic formulas, but that fact strengthens the case for their inclusion, for opportunities to experience a Vespers service or Mass sung in Latin in their classic formulations are rare indeed. I decided to reproduce the editions of the modern chant books, with their stylized neumatic notation, despite the fact that they are not *urtexts,* because these books are the only resources many students will have available for this repertory, and it should be part of their training to become familiar with the editorial conventions of the Solesmes editions.

These volumes of music do not contain any commentaries, because only an extended essay would have done justice to each of the selections. By leaving interpretation to students and teachers, I hope to enrich their opportunities for research and analysis, for discovery and appreciation. Another reason for not accompanying the music with critical and analytical notes is that this anthology was conceived as a companion to Donald J. Grout's *A History of Western Music,* the Fourth Edition of which I revised. Brief discussions of every number in this collection will be found in that book: some barely scratch the surface, others are extended analytical and historical reflections. An index to these discussions by number in this anthology is at the back of each volume.

The anthology, it must be emphasized, was intended to stand by itself as a selection of music representing every important trend, genre, national school and historical development or innovation. It is accompanied by both records and cassettes.

The translations of the poetic and prose texts are my own except where acknowledged. They are literal to a fault, corresponding to the original line by line, if not word for word, with consequent inevitable damage to the English style. I felt that the musical analyst prefers precise detail concerning the text that the composer had before him rather than imaginative and evocative writing. I am indebted to Ann Walters for helping with some stubborn medieval Latin poems and to Ingeborg Glier for casting light on what seemed to me some impenetrable lines of middle-high German.

A number of research assistants, all at one time students at Yale, shared in the background research, in many of the routine tasks, as well as in some of the joys of discovery and critical selection. Robert Ford and Carolyn Abbate explored options in pre-Baroque and post-Classical music respectively during the selection phase. Gail Hilson Wulder and Kenneth Suzuki surveyed the literature on a sizeable number of the items, while Susan Cox Carlson contributed her expertise in early polyphony. Clara Marvin assisted in manifold ways in the last stages of this compilation.

My colleagues at Yale were generous with their advice on selections, particularly Elizabeth Keitel on Machaut, Craig Wright on Dufay, Leon Plantinga on Clementi, John Kirkpatrick on Ives, and Allen Forte on Schoenberg. Leeman Perkins' and Edward Roesner's suggestions after seeing preliminary drafts of the Medieval and Renaissance sections contributed to rounding out those repertories. I am also indebted to Paul Henry Lang for his reactions to the classic period choices and to Christoph Wolff for those of the Baroque period.

The Yale Music Library was the indispensable base of operations, and its staff a prime resource for the development of this anthology. I wish to thank particularly Harold Samuel, Music Librarian, and his associates Alfred B. Kuhn, Kathleen J. Moretto, Karl W. Schrom, Kathryn R. Mansi, and Deborah Miller for their many favors to me and my assistants.

Most of all I have to thank Claire Brook, whose idea it was to compile an anthology to accompany the Third and Fourth Editions of *A History of Western Music.* Her foresight, intuition, and creative editorial style gave me confidence that somehow within a short space of time this complex enterprise would unfold. Thanks to the efforts of her assistant, Ray Morse, we were able to achieve the goal of bringing out the anthology with the accompanying text.

From my first association with this project, Professor Grout's text set a standard of quality and scope that was my constant challenge and inspiration. He accepted the idea of the anthology with enthusiasm and subordinated proprietary and justly prideful feelings to a pedagogical ideal. For this, the users of these tools and I owe him a great debt, particularly since this coupling of text and anthology has already achieved a measure of the success that his book has enjoyed.

W. W. Norton and I are grateful to the individuals and publishers cited in the footnotes who granted permission to reprint, re-edit or adapt material under copyright. Where no modern publication is cited, the music was edited from original sources.

Claude V. Palisca
Hamden, Connecticut

Norton Anthology of
WESTERN MUSIC

SECOND EDITION

VOLUME I

Medieval • Renaissance • Baroque

Euripides (ca. 485–ca. 406 B. C.)
Orestes (408 B. C.), *Stasimon* chorus, fragment, lines 338–44.
Music by Euripides (?). Papyrus (ca. 200 B. C.)

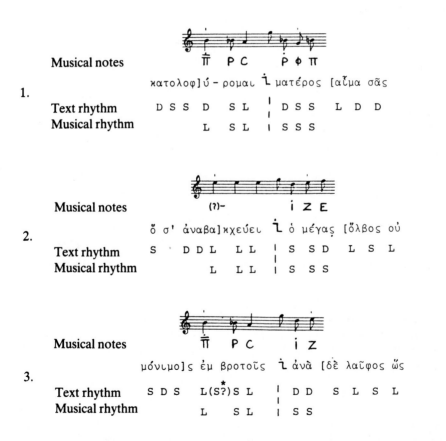

Vienna, Österreichische Nationalbibliothek, Papyrus G2315. Analytical transcription by Thomas J. Mathiesen in "Rhythm and Meter in Ancient Greek Music," *Music Theory Spectrum* 7 (1985):177.

4.

Musical notes	C P π̄	C P	ἰ φ C –

τι]ς ἀκάτου θοᾶς   τινά[ξας δαίμων

Text rhythm	D	D D L	SL	D L L	L L
Musical rhythm		S S L	SL	S L	

5.

Musical notes	φ̇ π ρ π̄

κατέκλυσεν ⁊ɔ ϲ ʟɔ   δ[εινῶν

Text rhythm	D C D S	L L
Musical rhythm	S S S L ⅄ S̲S̲	

6.

Musical notes	Z̊ ί Z

πόνω]ν ⁊ɔ ϲ ʟɔ ὡὼς πόντ[ου

Text rhythm	S L	L	L L
Musical rhythm	⅄ S̲_S̲	SS	L

7.

Musical notes	· C̊ P Z̲

[text uncertain]

*on the special function of the mu in syllabic quantity, see Aristides Quintilianus 1.21.

D = dichronic syllable | = possible position of the thesis
S = short syllable
L = long syllable
C = common syllable

You wild goddesses who dart across the skies seeking vengeance for murder, we implore you to free Agamemnon's son from his raging fury. . . . We grieve for this boy. Happiness is brief among mortals. Sorrow and anguish sweep down on it like a swift gust of wind on a sloop, and it sinks under the tossing seas.

Epitaph of Seikilos
Tomb stele, Tralles, Asia Minor,
ca. second century B. C.

1.

Musical notes   C Z̄ Z̈ ĸ ɪ z ꞇ

"Όσον ζῆς φαί — νου

Text rhythm	S	L	L	L		L
Musical rhythm	S	L	L+S	S	S	S L+S

2.

Musical notes   ĸ̄ ɪ Ż ɪ̲ ĸ ō C o‿φ̈

μηδὲν ὅλ–ως σὺ λυ–ποῦ·

Text rhythm	L	S	S	L	D	D	L
Musical rhythm	L	S	S	SS	S	L	S+L

3.

Musical notes   C ĸ Ż ɪ̇ ĸ̇ ɪ ĸ C̄ o φ̈

πρὸς ὀλίγον ἐ—στὶ τὸ ζῆν,

Text rhythm	S	S	D	S	L	D	S	L
Musical rhythm	S	S	S	S	SS	S	L	S+L

4.

Musical notes   C ĸ O ɪ̇ Ż ĸ C C̄   C X̄ꞇ

τὸ τέλος ὀ χρόνος ἀ παι– τεῖ.

Text rhythm	S	S	S	C	S	S	D	L	L
Musical rhythm	S	S	S	S	S	S	S	L	S+L

D = dichronic syllable | = possible position of the thesis

S = short syllable   C = common syllable   L = long syllable

As long as you live, be lighthearted. Let nothing trouble you.
Life is only too short, and time takes its toll.

Copenhagen, National Museum, Inventory No. 14897 (for photograph, see Grout-Palisca, *History of Western Music*, p. 19). Analytical transcription by Thomas J. Mathiesen in "Rhythm and Meter in Ancient Greek Music," *Music Theory Spectrum* 7 (1985):171–72

Mass for Septuagesima Sunday

Instructions for reading modern plainchant notation.

One line of the four-line staff is designated by a clef as either middle C (𝄡) or the F immediately below it (𝄢). These are not absolute but relative pitches. The *neumes,* as the shapes are called, are usually assigned equal durations, although at one time they may have had some temporal significance. Two or more neumes in succession on the same line or space, if on the same syllable, are sung as though tied. Composite neumes, representing two or more pitches, are read from left to right, except for the *podatus* or *pes* (𝄪), in which the lower note is sung first. Oblique neumes (◥) stand for two different pitches. A neume, whether simple or composite, never carries more than one syllable. Flat signs, except in a signature at the beginning of a line, are valid only until the next vertical division line or until the beginning of the next word.

The Vatican editions, such as the *Liber Usualis* (*LU*), employ, in addition a number of interpretive signs, based on the performance practices of the Benedictine monks of the Solesmes Congregation. A horizontal dash above or below a neume means it is to be slightly lengthened. A vertical stroke above or below a note marks the beginning of a rhythmic unit when this would not otherwise be obvious. A dot after a note doubles its value. Vertical bars of varied lengths show the division of a melody into periods (full bar), phrases (half-bar), and smaller members (a stroke through the uppermost staff-line). The note-like symbol on a space or line at the end of the staff is a *custos* (guard), a guide to lead the reader to the first note on the following line.

An asterisk in the text shows where the chorus takes over from the soloist, and the signs *ij* and *iij* (ditto and double–ditto) indicate that the preceding phrase is to be sung twice or three times.

a) Introit, *Circumdederunt me*

Intr. 5.

Ⅽircumdedé-runt me * gémi-tus mórtis, do-ló- res
inférni circum-de- dé- runt me : et in tri- bu-la-
ti- ó-ne mé- a invo- cá- vi Dóminum, et exaudí-

Ordinaries from Mass XI, *LU,* pp. 46–48; propers from *LU,* 497–501.

vit de témplo sáncto sú- o vó- cem mé- am.

Ps. Dí-ligam te Dómine, forti-túdo mé- a : * Dóminus firma-

méntum mé-um, et re-fúgi-um mé- um, et liberá-tor mé-us.

Gló-ri- a Pátri. E u o u a e.

Repeat Introit, *Circumdederunt me . . . vocem meam.*

b) *Kyrie*

(x) XIV-XVI. c.

1.

Ḱ Y-ri- e * e- lé- i-son. *iij.* Chríste

e- lé- i-son. *iij.* Ký-ri- e e- lé- i-son. *ij.* Ký-

ri- e * e- lé- i-son.

(The *Gloria in excelsis* is not sung from Septuagesima Sunday until Easter, except on Maundy Thursday, Holy Saturday, and Feast days).

c) Collect

Pre-ces po-pu-li tu-i, quae-su-mus Do-mi-ne, cle-men-ter e-xau-di: et qui ju-ste pro

pec-ca-tis nos-stris af-fli-gi-mur, pro tui no-mi-nis glo-ri-a mi-se-ri-cor-di-ter li-be-re-mur.

Per Do-mi-num nos-trum Je-sum Chri-stum Fi-li-um tu-um: qui te-cum vi-vit et re-gnat in

u-ni-ta-te Spi-ri-tus Sanc-ti De-us,   per om-ni-a sae-cu-la sae-cu-lo-rum. R̸. A-men.

d) Epistle

[Full stop]

Lec-ti-o E-pi-sto-lae be-a-ti Pau-li A-po-sto-li   ad Co-rin-thi-os.   Fra-tres:

[Interrogation]

Ne-sci-tis quod i-i qui in sta-di-o cur-runt, om-nes qui-dem cur-runt, sed u-nus ac-ci-pit bra-vi-um?

Sic cur-ri-te, ut com-pre-hen-da-tis.   Om-nis-au-tem, qui in a-go-ne con-ten-dit ab

[Metrum]

om-ni-bus se ab-sti-net: et il-li qui-dem ut cor-rup-ti-bi-lem co-ro-nam ac-ci-pi-ant;

nos au-tem in-cor-rup-tam. E-go i-gi-tur sic cur-ro, non qua-si in in-cer-tum: sic pu-gno,

non qua-si ae-rem ver-be-rans: sed ca-sti-go cor-pus me-um, et in ser-vi-tu-tem red-i-go:

ne for-te cum a-li-is prae-di-ca-ve-rim, ip-se re-pro-bus ef-fi-ci-ar.   No-lo e-nim vos

i-gno-ra-re, fra-tres,   quo-ni-am pa-tres no-stri om-nes sub nu-be fu-e-runt,   et om-nes

ma-re tran-si-e-runt, et om-nes in Mo-y-se bap-ti-za-ti sunt in nu-be, et in ma-ri:

et om-nes e-am-dem es-cam spi-ri-ta-lem man-du-ca-ve-runt. et om-nes eum-dem po-tum

spi-ri-ta-lem bi-be-runt: (bi-be-bant au-tem de spi-ri-ta-li, con-se-quen-te e-os, pe-tra:

pe-tra au-tem e-rat Chri-stus) sed non in plu-ri-bus e-o-rum be-ne-pla-ci-tum est De-o.

e) Gradual, *Adjutor in opportunitatibus*

Grad. 3.

A Djú- tor * in opportu-ni- tá- ti- bus,

in tri- bu-la-ti- ó- ne : spé- rent in te,

qui nové-runt te : quó-ni- am non dere-

línquis quae- réntes te, Dó- mi- ne.

℣. Quó-ni- am non

in fí-nem oblí- vi- o é- rit páupe- ris :

pa-ti- énti- a páu- pe- rum non per-í- bit in ae-tér-

num : exsúrge, Dómi- ne, non praevá- le-

at * hó- mo.

f) Tract, *De profundis clamavi*

Tract. 8.

DE profún- dis * clamá-vi ad te, Dómi- ne :

Dómi- ne, exáu-di vó- cem

mé- am. ℣. Fí- ant áures tú- ae

in- tendén- tes in o-

ra- ti- ó- nem sér- vi tú-

i. ℣. Si in-iquitá-tes ob-servá- ve-ris, Dó- mi-

ne : Dómi- ne, quis sus- tiné-

bit? ℣. Qui-a apud te pro-pi-ti- á-ti-

o est, et propter lé- gem tú-

am sustí- nu- i te, * Dómine.

g) Gospel

[Metrum]

Do-mi-nus vo-bis-cum. R̸. Et cum spi-ri-tu tu-o.   Se-quen-ti-a san-cti E-van-ge-li-i

[Full stop]

se-cun-dum Mat-thae-um.   R̸. Glo-ri-a   ti-bi Do-mi-ne.   In il-lo tem-po-re:

Di-xit Je-sus di-sci-pu-lis su-is pa-ra-bo-lam hanc: Si-mi-le est re-gnum

cae-lo-rum ho-mi-ni pa-tri-fa-mi-li-as,   qui e-xi-it pri-mo ma-ne con-du-ce-re

[Conclusion]

o-pe-ra-ri-o in vi-ne-am su-am ... Mul-ti e-nim sunt vo-ca-ti,   pau-ci ve-ro e-lec-ti.

h) *Credo*

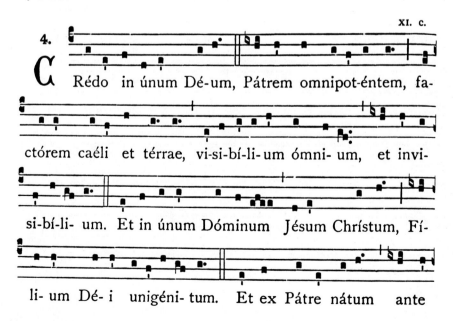

XI. c.

4.

C Rédo in únum Dé-um, Pátrem omnipot-éntem, fa-

ctórem caéli et térrae, vi-si-bí-li-um ómni-um, et invi-

si-bí-li-um. Et in únum Dóminum Jésum Chrístum, Fí-

li-um Dé-i unigéni-tum. Et ex Pátre nátum   ante

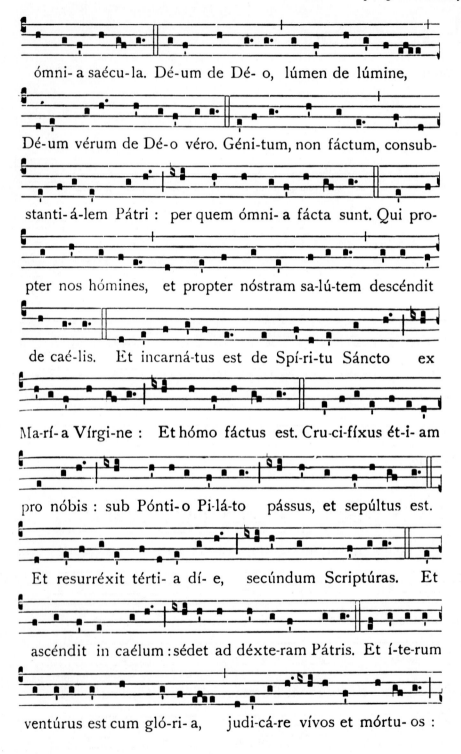

ómni- a saécu- la. Dé-um de Dé- o, lúmen de lúmine,

Dé-um vérum de Dé-o véro. Géni-tum, non fáctum, consub-

stanti-á-lem Pátri : per quem ómni- a fácta sunt. Qui pro-

pter nos hómines, et propter nóstram sa-lú-tem descéndit

de caé-lis. Et incarná-tus est de Spí-ri-tu Sáncto ex

Ma-rí- a Vírgi-ne : Et hómo fáctus est. Cru-ci-fíxus ét-i- am

pro nóbis : sub Pónti- o Pi-lá-to pássus, et sepúltus est.

Et resurréxit térti- a dí- e, secúndum Scriptúras. Et

ascéndit in caélum : sédet ad déxte-ram Pátris. Et í-te-rum

ventúrus est cum gló-ri- a, judi-cá-re vívos et mórtu- os :

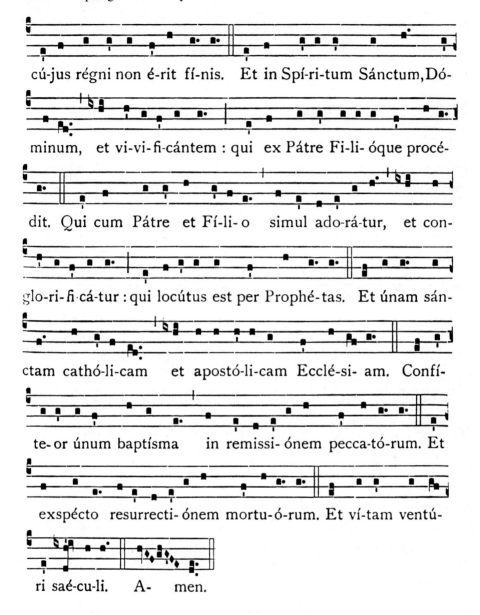

cú-jus régni non é-rit fí-nis. Et in Spí-ri-tum Sánctum,Dó-

minum, et vi-vi-fi-cántem : qui ex Pátre Fi-li- óque procé-

dit. Qui cum Pátre et Fí-li- o simul ado-rá-tur, et con-

glo-ri-fi-cá-tur : qui locútus est per Prophé-tas. Et únam sán-

ctam cathó-li-cam et apostó-li-cam Ecclé-si- am. Confí-

te- or únum baptísma in remissi- ónem pecca-tó-rum. Et

exspécto resurrecti- ónem mortu-ó-rum. Et ví-tam ventú-

ri saé-cu-li. A- men.

i) Offertory, *Bonum est confiteri*

Offert.
8.
B Onum est * confi-té- ri Dómi- no, et

psál- le- re   nó- mi- ni tú-   o,   Al-tíssi-

me.

(Preface omitted)

j) *Sanctus*

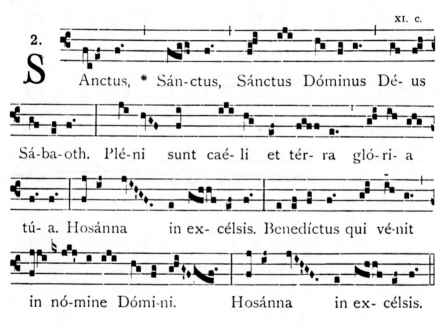

Anctus, * Sán-ctus, Sánctus Dóminus Dé- us

Sá-ba-oth. Plé-ni   sunt caé- li   et tér- ra gló-ri- a

tú- a. Hosánna   in ex- célsis. Benedíctus qui vé-nit

in nó-mine Dómi-ni.   Hosánna   in ex- célsis.

(*Pater noster* omitted)

k) *Agnus Dei*

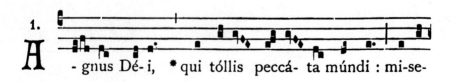

- gnus Dé- i, * qui tóllis peccá- ta múndi : mi-se-

ré-re nóbis.   Agnus Dé- i, *qui tól- lis peccá-ta mún-

di : mi-se-ré-re nóbis.   Agnus Dé- i, *qui tóllis pec-cá- ta

múndi :   dóna nóbis pácem.

l) Communion, *Illumina faciem tuam*

Comm.
1.

Llú-mi-na * fá-ci-em tú-am super sérvum tú- um,

et sálvum me   fac   in tú-   a mi- se-ri-córdi-   a :

Dó-mine, non confúndar,   quó-ni- am invo- cá- vi te.

(*Post Communion* omitted)

m) *Benedicamus Domino*

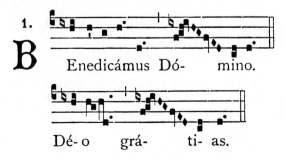

1.

B   Enedicámus Dó-   mino.

Dé- o   grá-   ti- as.

Introit

Ps. 17. 5, 6, 7, 2-3

Circumdederunt me gemitus mortis, dolores inferni circumdederunt me: et in tribulatione mea invocavi Dominum, et exaudivit de templo sancto suo vocem meam. *Ps.* Diligam te, Domine, fortitudo mea: Dominus firmamentum meum, et refugium meum, et liberator meus. ℣. Gloria Patri.

The groans of death surround me, the sorrows of hell encompassed me: and in my affliction I called upon the Lord, and He heard my voice, from His holy temple. *Ps. 17, 2, 3.* I will love Thee, O Lord, my strength: the Lord is my firmament, and my refuge and my deliverer. ℣. Glory.

Kyrie

Kyrie eleison.
Christe eleison.
Kyrie eleison.

Lord have mercy.
Christ have mercy.
Lord have mercy.

Collect

Preces populi tui, quaesumus, Domine, clementer exaudi: ut, qui juste pro peccatis nostris affligimur, pro tui nominis gloria misericorditer liberemur. Per Dominum.

Do Thou, we beseech Thee, O Lord, graciously hear the prayers of Thy people, that we, who are justly afflicted for our sins, may be mercifully delivered for the glory of Thy name. Through our Lord.

Epistle

1 Cor. 9, 24–27; 10, 1–5

Lectio Epistolae beati Pauli Apostoli ad Corinthos.

Fratres: Nescitis quod ii qui in stadio currunt, omnes quidem currunt, sed unus accipit bravium? Sic currite, ut comprehendatis. Omnis autem qui in agone contendit, ab omnibus se abstinet: et illi quidem ut corruptibilem coronam accipiant; nos autem incorruptam. Ego igitur sic curro, non quasi in incertum: sic pugno, non quasi aerem verberans: sed castigo corpus meum, et in servitutem redigo: ne forte cum aliis praedicaverim, ipse reprobus efficiar. Nolo enim vos ignorare, fratres, quoniam patres nostri omnes sub nube fuerunt, et omnes mare transierunt, et omnes in Moyse baptizati sunt in nube, et in mari: et omnes eamdem escam spiritalem manducaverunt, et omnes eumdem potum spiritalem biberunt: (bibebant autem de spiritali, consequente eos, petra: petra autem erat Christus): sed non in pluribus eorum beneplacitum est Deo.

Lesson from the Epistle of blessed Paul the Apostle to the Corinthians.

Brethren, know you not that they that run in the race, all run indeed, but one receiveth the prize? So run, that you may obtain. And every one that striveth for the mastery, refraineth himself from all things: and they indeed that they may receive a corruptible crown, but we an incorruptible one. I therefore so run, not as at an uncertainty; I so fight, not as one beating the air: but I chastise my body, and bring it into subjection: lest perhaps, when I have preached to others, I myself should become a castaway. For I would not have you ignorant, brethren, that our fathers were all under the cloud, and all passed through the sea; and all in Moses were baptized, in the cloud and in the sea; and all did eat the same spiritual food, and all drank the same spiritual drink; (and they drank of the spiritual rock that followed them; and the rock was Christ). But with the most of them God was not well pleased.

Text and translation from F. X. Lasance and F. A. Walsh, *The New Roman Missal*. (New York: Benziger Press, 1950). Reprinted by permission.

Gradual

Ps. 9. 10–11, 19–20

Adjutor in opportunitatibus, in tribulatione: sperent in te, qui noverunt te: quoniam non derelinquis quaerentes te, Domine. ℣. Quoniam non in finem oblivio erit pauperis: patientia pauperum non peribit in aeternum: exsurge, Domine non praevaleat homo.

The helper in due time, in tribulation: let them trust in Thee, who know Thee: for Thou dost not forsake them that seek Thee, O Lord. *V.* For the poor man shall not be forgotten to the end: the patience of the poor shall not perish for ever: arise, O Lord, let not man be strengthened.

Tract

Ps. 129. 1–4

De profundis clamavi ad te, Domine: Domine, exaudi vocem meam. ℣. Fiant aures tuae intendentes in orationem servi tui. ℣. Si iniquitates observaveris, Domine: Domine, quis sustinebit? ℣. Quia apud te propitiatio est, et propter legem tuam sustinui te, Domine.

From the depths I have cried to Thee, O Lord; Lord, hear my voice. ℣. Let Thine ears be attentive to the prayer of Thy servant. ℣. If Thou shalt observe iniquities, O Lord, Lord, Who shall endure it? ℣. For with Thee is propitiation, and by reason of Thy law I have waited for Thee, O Lord.

Gospel

In illo tempore: Dixit Jesus discipulis suis parabolam hanc: Simile est regnum caelorum homini patrifamilias, qui exiit primo mane conducere operarios in vineam suam. Conventione autem facta cum operariis ex denario diurno, misit eos in vineam suam. Et egressus circa horam tertiam, vidit alios stantes in foro otiosos, et dixit illis: Ite et vos in vineam meam, et quod justum fuerit, dabo vobis. Illi autem abierunt. Iterum autem exiit circa sextam et nonam horam: et fecit similiter. Circa undecimam vero exiit, et invenit alios stantes, et dicit illis: Quid hic statis ota die otiosi? Dicunt ei: Quia nemo nos conduxit. Dicit illis: Ite et vos in vineam meam. Cum sero autem factum esset, dicit dominus vineae procuratori suo: Voca operarios, et redde illis mercedem, incipiens a novissimis usque ad primos. Cum venissent ergo qui circa undecimam horam venerant, acceperunt singulos denarios. Venientes autem et primi, arbitrati sunt quod plus essent accepturi: acceperunt autem et ipsi singulos denarios. Et accipientes murmurabant adversus patremfamilias, dicentes: Hi novissimi una hora fecerunt, et pares illos nobis fecisti, qui portavimus pondus diei, et aestus. At ille respondens uni eorum, dixit: Amice,

At that time, Jesus spoke to His disciples this parable: The kingdom of heaven is like to a householder, who went out early in the morning to hire laborers into his vineyard. And having agreed with the laborers for a penny a day, he sent them into his vineyard. And going out about the third hour, he saw others standing in the marketplace idle, and he said to them, Go you also into my vineyard, and I will give you what shall be just: and they went their way. And again he went out about the sixth and the ninth hour, and did in like manner. But about the eleventh hour, he went out, and found others standing; and he saith to them, Why stand you here all the day idle? They say to him, Because no man hath hired us. He saith to them, Go you also into my vineyard. And when evening was come, the lord of the vineyard saith to his steward, Call the laborers, and pay them their hire, beginning from the last even to the first. When therefore they were come that came about the eleventh hour, they received every man a penny. But when the first also came, they thought that they should receive more; and they also received every man a penny. And receiving it, they murmured against the master of the house,

non facio tibi injuriam: nonne ex denario convenisti mecum? Tolle quod tuum est, et vade: volo autem et huic novissimo dare sicut et tibi. Aut non licet mihi quod volo facere? an oculus tuus nequam est, quia ego bonus sum? Sic erunt novissimi primi, et primi novissimi. Multi enim sunt vocati, pauci vero electi.

saying, These last have worked but one hour, and thou hast made them equal to us that have borne the burden of the day and the heat. But he answering, said to one of them, Friend, I do thee no wrong; didst thou not agree with me for a penny? Take what is thine, and go thy way: I will also give to this last even as to thee. Or, is it not lawful for me to do what I will? is thy eye evil, because I am good? So shall the last be first, and the first last. For many are called, but few are chosen.

Credo

Credo in unum Deum, Patrem omnipotentem, factorem caeli et terrae, visibilium omnium et invisibilium. Et in unum Dominum Jesum Christum Filium Dei unigenitum. Et ex Patre natum ante omnia saecula. Deum de Deo, lumen de lumine, Deum verum de Deo vero. Genitum, non factum, consubstantialem Patri: per quem omnia facta sunt. Qui propter nos homines et propter nostram salutem descendit de caelis. Et incarnatus est de Spiritu Sancto ex Maria Virgine: et homo factus est. Crucifixus etiam pro nobis: sub Pontio Pilato passus, et sepultus est. Et resurrexit tertia die, secundum Scripturas. Et ascendit in caelum sedet ad dexteram Patris. Et iterum venturus est cum gloria judicare vivos et mortuos: cujus regni non erit finis. Et in Spiritum Sanctum, Dominum et vivicantem: qui ex Patre, Filioque procedit. Qui cum Patre, et Filio simul adoratur, et conglorificatur: qui locutus est per Prophetas. Et unam sanctam catholicam et apostolicam Ecclesiam. Confiteor unum baptisma in remissionem peccatorum. Et expecti resurrectionem mortuorum Et vitam venturi saeculi. Amen.

I believe in one God, Father almighty, maker of heaven and earth and of all things visible and invisible. And in one Lord Jesus Christ, the only-begotten Son of God, born of the Father before all ages. God of God, light of light, true God of true God. Begotten, not made, being of one substance with the Father, by whom all things were made. Who for us men and for our salvation came down from heaven. And was made incarnate by the Holy Ghost of the Virgin Mary, and was made man. And was crucified for us under Pontius Pilate. He suffered and was buried. And the third day he rose again according to the Scriptures. And ascended into heaven, and sitteth on the right hand of the Father. And he shall come again with glory to judge the quick and the dead; of whose kingdom there shall be no end. And in the Holy Ghost, Lord and giver of life, who proceedeth from the Father and the Son. Who, together with the Father and the Son, is worshiped and glorified; who spake by the prophets. And one holy, Catholic, and Apostolic Church. I acknowledge one baptism for the remission of sins. And I look for the resurrection of the dead, and the life of the world to come. Amen.

Offertory

Ps. 91, 2

Bonum est confiteri Domino, et psallere nomini tuo, Altissime.

It is good to give praise to the Lord, and to sing to Thy name, O Most High.

Sanctus

Sanctus, Sanctus, Sanctus Dominus Deus Sabaoth. Pleni sunt caeli et terra gloria tua. Hosanna in excelsis. Benedictus qui venit in nomine Domini. Hosanna in excelsis. [Canon] Per omnia saecula saeculorum. R Amen.

Holy, holy, holy, Lord God of Hosts. The heavens and earth are full of thy glory. Hosanna in the highest. Blessed is he who comes in the name of the Lord. Hosanna in the highest. [Canon] World without end, Rx Amen.

Agnus Dei

Agnus Dei, qui tollis peccata mundi: miserere nobis. Agnus Dei, qui tollis peccata mundi: miserere nobis. Agnus Dei, qui tollis peccata mundi: dona nobis pacem.

Lamb of God, who takest away the sins of the world, have mercy on us. Lamb of God, who takest away the sins of the world, have mercy on us. Lamb of God, who takest away the sins of the world, give us peace.

Communion

Ps. 30. 17–18

Illumina faciem tuam super servum tuum, et salvum me fac in tua misericordia: Domine, non confundar, quoniam invocavi te.

Make Thy face to shine upon Thy servant, and save me in Thy mercy: Let me not be confounded, O Lord, for I have called upon Thee.

Benedicamus Domino

Benedicamus Domino.
Deo gratias.

Let us bless the Lord.
Thanks be to God.

Office of Second Vespers,
Nativity of Our Lord

a) Verse, *Deus in Adjutorium*

℣. **D** E-us in adjutó-ri- um mé- um inténde. ℟. Dómine ad adju-

vándum me festí-na. Gló-ri- a Pátri, et Fí-li- o, et Spi- rí-tu- i Sán-

cto. Sic-ut érat in princípi- o, et nunc, et semper, et in saécu-la

saecu-ló-rum. Amen. Alle-lú-ia.

b) Antiphon, *Tecum principium*

T ECUM prin-cí- pi- um * in di- e virtú-tis

The Chapter, *Kyrie, Pater noster,* and Prayer (*Oratio*) have been omitted. Antiphons, Short Responsory and Verse *Notum fecit* from *AM*, pp. 245–49. *Deus in adjutorium: LU*, p. 112; Psalm 109: *LU*, p. 128, Tone lg; Psalm 110: *LU*, p. 132, Tone 7a; Psalm 111: *LU*, p. 146, Tone 7d; Psalm 129: *LU*, p. 130, Tone 4a; *Magnificat: LU*, p. 213, Tone 1g².

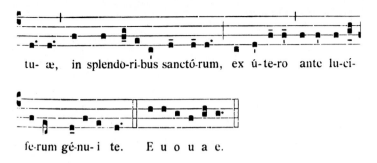

tu- æ, in splendò-ri-bus sanctó-rum, ex ú-te-ro ante lu-cí-

fe-rum gé-nu- i te.   E u o u a e.

c) Psalm 109, *Dixit Dominus*

A model for realizing the psalm formula is given for Psalm 110.

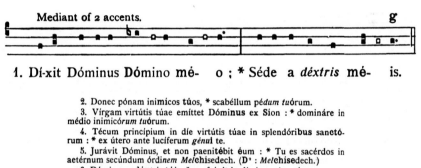

Mediant of 2 accents.   **g**

1. Dí-xit Dóminus Dómino mé-   o ; * Séde a *déxtris* mé-   is.

2. Donec pónam inimicos túos, * scabéllum pé*dum tu*órum.
3. Vírgam virtútis túae emíttet Dóminus ex Sion : * domináre in médio inimicó*rum tu*órum.
4. Técum princípium in díe virtútis túae in splendóribus sanctó-rum : * ex útero ante lucíferum gé*nu*i te.
5. Jurávit Dóminus, et non paenitébit éum : * Tu es sacérdos in aetérnum secúndum órdi*nem Melc*hisedech. (D² : *Melc*hisedech.)
6. Dóminus a déxtris túis, * confrégit in díe irae sú*ae* réges.
7. Judicábit in natiónibus, implébit ruínas : * conquassábit cápita in térra mul*t*órum.
8. De torrénte in via bibet : * proptérea exal*tábit* cáput.
9. Glória Pátri, et Filio, * et Spirí*tui* Sáncto.
10. Sicut érat in princípio, et núnc, et sémper, * et in saécula saecu-*lórum*. Amen.

Return to Antiphon, *Tecum principium*

d) Antiphon, *Redemptionem misit Dominus*

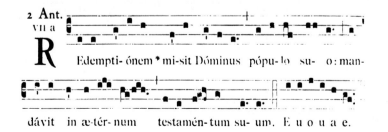

2 Ant.
vii a

R Edempti- ónem * mi-sit Dóminus pópu- lo su- o : man-

dávit in æ-tér- num   testamén-tum su- um. E u o u a e.

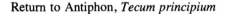

e) Psalm 110, *Confitebor tibi Domine*

Intonation   Tenor   Mediant of 2 accents

1. Con - fi - te - bor ti - bi Do-mi - ne in to - to   cor - de me - o:
2.   Ma - gna   o - pe - ra Do - mi - ni
3.   Con-fes - si - o et ma- gni - fi - cen - ti - a   o - pus e - jus:

Flex

4. Me - mo - ri - am fe - cit mi - ra - bi - li - um su - o - rum, †

   mi - se - ri - cors et mi - se -   ra - tor Do - mi - nus:
5. Me - mor e - rit in sae - cu - lum tes - ta -   men - ti su - i:
6. Ut det il - lis hae - re - di -   ta - tem gen - ti - um:

Flex

7. Fi - de - li - a om - ni - a man - da - ta   e - jus: †

   con - fir - ma - ta in   sae - cu - lum sae - cu - li:
8. Re-demp-ti - o-nem mi - sit po -   pu   lo su - o:
9. Sanc-tum et ter - ri - bi - le   no - men e - jus:
10. In - tel - lec - tus bo-nus om - ni - bus fa - ci - en - ti - bus e - um:
11. Glo - ri - a Pa -   tri   et Fi - li - o,
12. Si - cut e - rat in prin - ci - pi - o, et   nunc,   et sem - per,

† This symbol in a psalm text calls for a Flex.

* This symbol in a psalm text marks the closing versicle, which is sung to the Tenor followed by the Termination

◻ The hollow note is sung when there are two unaccented syllables after the accented one, as in *ó-pe-ra Dó-mi-ni*.

f) Antiphon, *Exortum est in tenebris*

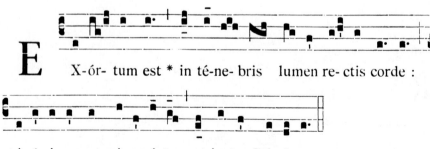

E X-ór- tum est * in té-ne- bris   lumen re- ctis corde :

mi-sé-ri-cors et mi-se-rá-tor, et justus Dómi-nus.

Tenor   Termination of 2 accents

1 *in con-si - li - o   ju - sto-rum, et con-gre -   ga   -   ti - o   -   ne.
2 *ex - qui-si - ta   in om-nes vo -lun -   ta   -   tes e   -   jus.
3 *et jus-ti - ti - a   e - jus ma -net in   sae - cu -lum sae - cu - li.

4 *es- cam de - dit ti -   men   -   ti - bus   se.

5 * vir - tu-tem o - pe -rum su - o-rum an -nun- ci - a- bit po- pu - lo   su   o.
6 * o - pe -ra   ma-nu - um   e - jus ve - ri - tas   et   ju - di - ci - um.

7* fac - ta in   ve - ri - ta - te et   ae   -   qui - ta   -   te.

8* man - da -vit   in ae - ter- num te -sta -   men - tum su   -   um.
9*   i - ni - ti - um sa - pi - en - ti - ae   ti   -   mor Do - mi - ni.
10* lau - da -tio   e - jus ma - net in   sae - cu - lum sae - cu - li.
11* et   Spi - ri -   tu   -   i   San   cto.
12* et   in sae - cu - la sae - cu -   lo   -   rum. A   -   men.

Return to Antiphon, *Redemptionem*

g) Psalm 111, *Beatus vir qui timet Dominum*

A model for realizing the psalm formula is given for Psalm 110.

Mediant of 2 accents   Endings of 2 accents   Flex

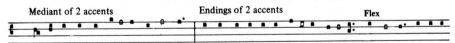

Be - á -tus vir qui ti - met Dó-mi-num: *in man-dá-tis é-jus vó - let ni - mis. cóm-mo-dat, †

2. Pótens in térra érit sé*men* éjus : * generátio rectórum be*nedice*̂tur.
3. Glória et divítiae in dó*mo* éjus : * et justítia éjus mánet in saé-*culum saé*culi.
4. Exórtum est in ténebris lú*men* r*éctis* : * miséricors, et miserá*tor, et* jùstus.
5. Jucúndus hómo qui miserétur et cómmodat, † dispónet sermónes súos in *judicio* : * quia in aetérnum non *commove*̂bitur.
6. In memória aetérna ér*it* jùstus : * ab auditióne mála *non time*̂bit.
7. Parátum cor éjus speráre in Dómino, † confirmátum est *cor* éjus : * non commovébitur donec despíciat inimícos sùos.

8. Dispérsit, dédit paupéribus : † justítia éjus mánet in saécu*lum* saéculi : * córnu éjus exaltábi*tur in* **gl**ória.

9. Peccátor vidébit, et irascétur, † déntibus súis frémet et *ta*béscet : * desidérium peccató*rum peri*bit.

10. Glória Pátri, *et* Fílio, * et Spirí*tui* Sáncto.

11. Sicut érat in princípio, et nunc, *et* sémper, * et in saécula saecu*lórum.* Amen.

Return to Antiphon, *Exortum*

h) Antiphon, *Apud Dominum*

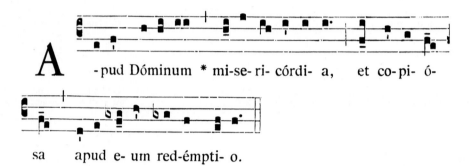

A -pud Dóminum * mi-se- ri- córdi- a,   et co-pi- ó-

sa   apud e- um red-émpti- o.

i) Psalm 129, *De profundis clamavi ad te*

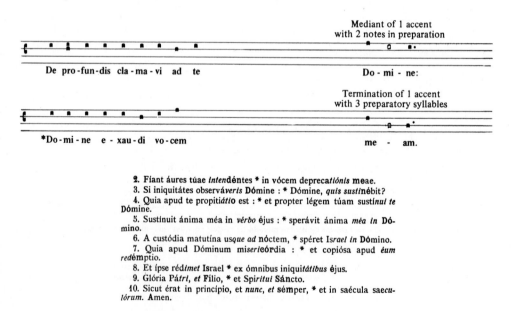

Mediant of 1 accent with 2 notes in preparation

De pro-fun-dis cla-ma-vi ad te   Do - mi - ne:

Termination of 1 accent with 3 preparatory syllables

*Do-mi-ne e - xau-di vo-cem   me - am.

2. Fíant áures túae *inten*déntes * in vócem depreca*tiónis* meae.

3. Si iniquitátes observá*veris* Dómine : * Dómine, *quis* susti*né*bit?

4. Quia apud te propitiá*tio* est : * et propter légem túam susti*nui te* Dómine.

5. Sustínuit ánima méa in *vérbo* éjus : * sperávit ánima *méa in* Dómino.

6. A custódia matutína us*que ad* nóctem, * spéret Is*rael in* Dómino.

7. Quia apud Dóminum miser*i*córdia : * et copiósa apud *éum* red*é*mptio.

8. Et ípse réd*imet* Israel * ex ómnibus iniqui*tátibus* éjus.

9. Glória Pá*tri, et* Fílio, * et Spirí*tui* Sáncto.

10. Sicut érat in princípio, et *nunc, et* sémper, * et in saécula saecu*lórum.* Amen.

Return to Antiphon, *Apud Dominum*

j) Short Responsory, *Verbum caro*

℟. br.
VI

VErbum ca- ro factum est, * Alle- lú- ia, al-

le- lú- ia. Verbum ca- ro factum est, * Alle- lú- ia,

al-le- lú- ia. ℣. Et ha-bi-tá-vit in no- bis.

* Alle- lú-ia. al- le- lú- ia. ℣. Gló-ri- a Patri, et Fí-

li- o, et Spi- rí- tu- i Sancto. Verbum ca- ro factum

est, * Alle- lú- ia, al- le- lú- ia.

k) Hymn, *Christe Redemptor omnium*

I

CHriste Red-émptor ómni- um, Ex Patre Patris ú- ni-

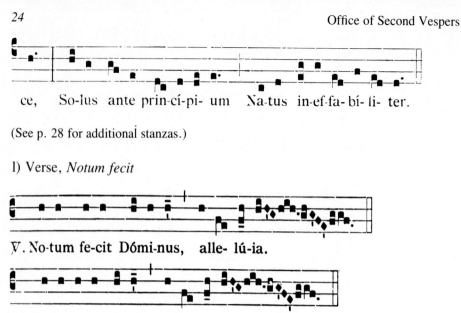

ce,   So-lus ante prin-cí-pi- um   Na-tus in-ef-fa- bí- li- ter.

(See p. 28 for additional stanzas.)

l) Verse, *Notum fecit*

℣. No-tum fe-cit Dómi-nus,   alle- lú-ia.

℟. Sa-lu-tá-re su- um,   alle- lú- ia.

m) Antiphon, *Hodie Christus natus est*

HOdi- e * Chri- stus na-tus est : hó-di- e Salvá-tor

appá-ru- it : hó-di- e in terra canunt Ange-li, lætán- tur Ar-

chánge- li : hó-di- e   exsúl- tant justi, di-céntes : Gló-ri-   a

in excélsis De- o,   alle- lú- ia.

n) Canticle, *Magnificat*

Mediant of **1** accent with **3** preparatory syllables (and an extra note in anticipation of the accent in dactylic cadences).

Endings of **1** accent with **2** preparatory syllables.

Tone I.   g²

1. Magní- fi-cat *   ánima *mé- a* **Dóminum**.
2. Et exsultávit *spí- ri-tus* **mé-** us * in Dé- o sa-lu- *tá-ri* **mé-**   o.

3. Quia respéxit humilitátem *ancillae* súae : * ecce enim ex hoc beátam me dícent ómnes genera*tió*nes.
4. Quia fécit míhi *mágna qui* pótens est : * et sánctum nó*men* éjus.
5. Et misericórdia éjus a progénie *in pro*génies * timénti*bus* éum.
6. Fécit poténtiam in *bráchio* súo : * dispérsit supérbos ménte córd*is* súi.
7. Depósuit po*téntes de* séde, * et exalt*ávit* húmiles.
8. Esuriéntes *implévit* bónis : * et dívites dimísit *in*ánes.
9. Suscépit Israel *púerum* súum, * recordátus misericórdi*ae* súae.
10. Sicut locútus est *ad pátres* nóstros, * Abraham et sémini éjus *in* saécula.
11. Glória *Pátri, et* Fílio, * et Spiritu*i* Sáncto.
12. Sicut érat in princípio, *et nunc, et* sémper, * et in saécula saecu-*lórum*. Amen.

Return to Antiphon, *Hodie Christus*

(*Kyrie* and *Pater noster* omitted.)

Verse

V. Deus, in adiutorium meum intende.
R. Domine, ad adiuvandum me festina.
Gloria Patri, et Filio, et Spiritui Sancto. Sicut erat in principio, et nunc, et semper, et in saecula saeculorum. Amen. Alleluia.

V. O God, come to my assistance.
R. O Lord, make haste to help me.
Glory be to the Father, and to the Son, and to the Holy Ghost. As it was in the beginning, is now and ever shall be, world without end. Amen. Alleluia.

Antiphon with Psalm 109

Tecum principium in die virtutis tuae in splendoribus sanctorum, ex utero ante luciferum genui te.

With Thee is the principality in the day of Thy strength in the brightness of the Saints, from the womb before the day star I begot Thee.

Dixit Dominus Domino meo: sede a dextris meis: Donec ponam inimicos tuos scabellum pedum tuorum.

Virgam virtutis tuae emittet Dominus ex Sion: dominare in medio inimicorum tuorum.

Tecum principium in die virtutis tuae in splendoribus sanctorum: ex utero ante luciferum genui te.

Iuravit, Dominus, et non poenitebit eum: Tu es sacerdos in aeternum secundum ordinem Melchisedech.

Dominus a dextris tuis, confregit in die irae suae reges.

Iudicabit in nationibus, implebit ruinas: conquassabit capita in terra multorum.

De torrente in via bibet: propterea exaltabit caput.

Gloria Patri, et Filio, et Spiritui Sancto.

Sicut erat in principio, et nunc, et semper, et in saecula saeculorum. Amen.

The Lord said unto my Lord: Sit Thou at My right hand. Until I make Thine enemies Thy footstool.

The Lord shall send the rod of Thy strength out of Sion: rule Thou in the midst of Thine enemies.

Thine shall be the dominion in the day of Thy power, amid the brightness of the saints: from the womb, before the day star have I begotten Thee.

The Lord hath sworn, and will not repent: Thou art a Priest for ever after the order of Melchisedech.

The Lord at Thy right hand shall strike through kings in the day of His wrath.

He shall judge among the heathen, He shall fill the places with dead bodies: He shall wound the heads over many countries.

He shall drink of the brook in the way: therefore shall he lift up his head.

Glory be to the Father, and to the Son, and to the Holy Ghost.

As it was in the beginning, is now, and ever shall be, world without end. Amen.

Antiphon with Psalm 110

Redemptionem misit Dominus populo suo, mandavit in aeternum testamentum suum.

Confitebor tibi, Domine, in toto corde meo: in consilio iustorum, et congregatione.

Magna opera Domini: exquisita in omnes voluntates eius.

Confessio et magnificentia opus eius: et iustitia eius manet in saeculum saeculi.

Memoriam fecit mirabilium suorum, misericors et miserator Dominus: escam dedit timentibus se.

Memor erit in saeculum testamenti sui: virtutem operum suorum annuntiabit populo suo:

Ut det illis haereditatem gentium: opera manuum eius veritas et iudicium.

Fidelia omnia mandata eius: confirmata in saeculum saeculi: facta in veritate et aequitate.

Redemptionem misit populo suo: mandavit in aeternum testamentum suum.

The Lord hath sent redemption to His people, He hath commanded His convenant for ever.

I will praise Thee, O Lord, with my whole heart: in the assembly of the upright, and in the congregation.

The works of the Lord are great, meet to serve for the doing of His will.

His work is honourable and glorious, and His righteousness endureth for ever.

He hath made a memorial of His wonderful works: the Lord is gracious and full of compassion. He hath given meat unto them that fear Him:

He will ever be mindful of His convenant. He will show His people the power of His works;

That He may give them the heritage of the heathen. The works of His hands are verity and judgment:

All His commandments are sure; they stand fast for ever and ever, being done in truth and uprightness.

He sent redemption unto His people: He hath commanded His covenant for ever:

Sanctum et terribile nomen eius: initium sapientiae timor Domini.

Holy and terrible is His name. The fear of the Lord is the beginning of wisdom:

Intellectus bonus omnibus facientibus eum: laudatio eius manet in saeculum saeculi.

A good understanding have all they that do His commandments: His praise endureth for ever.

Gloria Patri, et Filio, et Spiritui Sancto.

Glory be to the Father, and to the Son, and to the Holy Ghost.

Sicut erat in principio, et nunc, et semper, et in saecula saeculorum. Amen.

As it was in the beginning, is now and ever shall be, world without end. Amen.

Antiphon with Psalm 111

Exortum est in tenebris lumen rectis corde: misericors, et miserator, et iustus Dominus.

To the true of heart a light is risen up in darkness: the Lord is merciful, and compassionate and just.

Beatus vir, qui timet Dominum: in mandatis eius volet nimis.

Blessed is the man that feareth the Lord, that delighteth greatly in His commandments.

Potens in terra erit semen eius: generatio rectorum benedicetur.

His seed shall be mighty upon earth; the generation of the upright shall be blessed.

Gloria et divitiae in dome eius: et iustitia eius manet in saeculum saeculi.

Glory and riches shall be in his house: and his righteousness endureth for ever.

Exortum est in tenebris lumen rectis: misericors, et miserator, et iustus.

Unto the upright there ariseth light in the darkness: he is gracious, and full of compassion, and righteousness.

Iucundus homo qui miseretur et commodat, disponent sermones suos in iudicio: quia in aeternum non commovebitur.

Happy is the man that showeth favour and lendeth; he will guide his words with discretion: surely he shall not be moved for ever.

In memoria aeterna erit iustus: ab auditione mala non timebit.

The righteous shall be in everlasting remembrance. He shall not be afraid of evil tidings.

Paratum cor eius sperare in Domino, confirmatum est cor eius: non commovebitur donec despiciat inimicos suos.

His heart is ready, trusting in the Lord. His heart is established, he shall not be afraid until he see his desire upon his enemies.

Dispersit, dedit pauperibus: iustitia eius manet in saeculum saeculi: cornu eius exaltabitur in gloria.

He hath dispersed, he hath given to the poor: his righteousness endureth for ever: his horn shall be exalted with honour.

Peccator videbit, et irascetur, dentibus suis fremet et tabescet: desiderium peccatorum peribit.

The wicked shall see it, and be grieved; he shall gnash his teeth, and melt away: the desire of the wicked shall perish.

Gloria Patri, et Filio, et Spiritui Sancto.

Glory be to the Father, and to the Son, and to the Holy Ghost.

Sicut erat in principio, et nunc et semper, et in saecula saeculorum. Amen.

As it was in the beginning, is now and ever shall be, world without end. Amen.

Antiphon with Psalm 129

Apud Dominum misericordia, et copiosa apud eum redemptio.

With the Lord there is mercy, and with Him plentiful redemption.

De profundis clamavi ad te, Domine: Domine, exaudi vocem meam.

Out of the depths I have cried to Thee, O Lord! Lord, hear my voice.

Fiant aures tuae intendentes: in vocem depre-
cationis meae.

Si iniquitates observaveris, Domine: Domine,
quis sustinebit?

Quia apud te propitiatio est: et propter legem
tuam sustinui te, Domine.

Sustinuit anima mea in verbo eius: speravit
anima mea in Domino.

A custodia matutina usque ad noctem: speret
Israel in Domino.

Quia apud Dominum misericordia: et copiosa
apud eum redemptio.

Et ipse redimet Israel, ex omnibus iniquita-
tibus eius.

Gloria Patri, et Filio, et Spiritui Sancto.

Sicut erat in principio, et nunc, et semper, et
in saecula saeculorum. Amen.

Let Thine ears be attentive to the voice of my
supplication.

If Thou, Lord, shalt observe iniquities, Lord,
who shall endure it?

For with Thee there is merciful forgiveness,
and by reason of Thy law I have waited
upon Thee, O Lord.

My soul hath relied on His word: my soul hath
hoped in the Lord.

From the morning watch even until night let
Israel hope in the Lord.

For with the Lord there is mercy, and with
Him plentiful redemption.

And He shall redeem Israel, from all his iniquities.

Glory be to the Father, and to the Son, and to
the Holy Ghost.

As it was in the beginning, is now and ever
shall be, world without end. Amen.

Short Responsory

R. Verbum caro factum est,
Alleluia, alleluia.
V. Et habitavit in nobis.
Alleluia, Alleluia.
Gloria Patri, et Filio
et Spiritui Sancto.

R. The Word was made flesh,
Alleluia, alleluia.
V. And dwelt among us.
Alleluia, alleluia.
Glory be to the Father, and to the Son,
and to the Holy Ghost.

Hymn

Christe, Redemptor omnium,
Ex Patre, Patris Unice,
Solus ante principium
Natus ineffabiliter

Jesus! Redeemer of the world!
Who, ere the earliest dawn of light,
Was from eternal ages born,
Immense in glory as in might.

Tu lumen, tu splendor Patris,
Tu spes perennis omnium:
Intende, quas fundunt preces.
Tui per orbem famuli.

Immortal Hope of all mankind
In whom the Father's face we see,
Hear Thou the prayers Thy people pour
This day throughout the world to Thee.

Memento, salutis Auctor,
Quod nostri quondam corporis,
Ex illibata Virgine
Nascendo, formam sumpseris.

Remember, O Creator Lord!
That in the Virgin's sacred womb
Thou was conceiv'd and of her flesh
Didst our mortality assume.

Sic praesens testatur dies,
Currens per anni circulum,
Quod solus a sede Patris
Mundi salus adveneris.

This ever-blest recurring day
Its witness bears, that all alone,
From Thy own Father's bosom forth,
To save the world Thou camest down.

Hunc caelum, terra, hunc mare,
Hunc omne, quod in eis est,

O Day! to which the seas and sky,
And earth, and heav'n, glad welcome sing;

Auctorem adventus tui
Laudans exultat cantico.

Nos quoque, qui sancto tuo,
Redempti sanguine sumus,
Ob diem natalis tui
Hymnum novum concinimus.

Gloria tibi, Domine,
Qui natus es de Virgine,
Cum Patre et Sancto Spiritu
In sempiterna saecula.

Amen

V. Notum fecit Dominus, alleluia.
R. Salutare suum, alleluia.

O Day! which heal'd our misery,
And brought on earth salvation's King.

We, too, O Lord, who have been cleans'd
In Thy own fount of Blood divine,
Offer the tribute of sweet song
On this blest natal day of Thine.

O Jesu! born of Virgin bright,
Immortal glory be to Thee;
Praise to the Father infinite
And Holy Ghost eternally.

Amen.

V. The Lord hath made known, alleluia.
R. His salvation, alleluia.

Antiphon at the Magnificat

Hodie Christus natus est: hodie Salvator apparuit:
hodie in terra canunt Angeli, laetantur Archangeli:
hodie exsultant iusti, dicentes:
Gloria in excelsis Deo, alleluia.

Magnificat anima mea Dominum.
Et exsultavit spiritus meus in Deo salutari meo.
Quia respexit humilitatem ancillae suae: ecce enim ex hoc beatam me dicent omnes generationes.
Quia fecit mihi magna qui potens est: et sanctum nomen eius.
Et misericordia eius a progenie in progenies timentibus eum.
Fecit potentiam in brachio suo: dispersit superbos mente cordis sui.

Deposuit potentes de sede, et exaltavit humiles.

Esurrentes implevit bonis: et divites dimisit inanes.
Suscepit Israel puerum suum, recordatus misericordiae suae.
Sicut locutus est ad patres nostros, Abraham, et semini eius in saecula.
Gloria Patri, et Filio et Spiritui Sancto.

Sicut erat in principio, et nunc, et semper, et in saecula saeculorum. Amen.

This day Christ was born: this day the Saviour appeared:
this day the Angels sing on earth, and the Archangels
rejoice: this day the just exult, saying:
Glory to God in the highest, alleluia.

My soul doth magnify the Lord.
And my spirit hath rejoiced in God my Saviour.
For He hath regarded the lowliness of His handmaid: for behold from henceforth all generations shall call me blessed.
For He that is mighty hath done great things to me: and holy is His name.
And His mercy is from generation unto generations, unto them that fear Him.
He hath showed strength with His arm: He hath scattered the proud in the imagination of their heart.

He hath put down the mighty from their seat, and hath exalted the humble.

He hath filled the hungry with good things: and the rich He hath sent empty away.
He hath received Israel His servant, being mindful of His mercy.
As He spake to our forefathers, Abraham and to his seed for ever.
Glory be to the Father, and to the Son, and to the Holy Ghost.

As it was in the beginning, is now and ever shall be, world without end. Amen.

Sequence for the Solemn Mass of Easter Day:

Victimae paschali laudes

Seq.
1. Vic - ti - mae pa - scha+li lau - des *im - mo - lent Chri - sti - a - ni.

2. A - gnus red - e - mit o - ves: Chri - stus in - no - cens Pa - tri re - con - ci - li - a - vit pec - ca - to - res.
3. Mors et vi - ta du - el + o con - fli - xe - re mi - ran - do: dux vi - tae mor - tu - us, re - gnat vi - vus.

4. Dic no - bis Ma - ri - a, quid vi - di - sti in vi - a?
5. An - ge - li - cos te - stes, su - da - ri - um, et ve - stes.

Se - pul - crum Chri - sti vi - ven - tis, et glo - ri - am vi - di re - sur - gen - tis:
Sur - re - xit Chri - stus spes me - a: prae - ce - det su - os in Ga - li - lae - am.

[6. Cre - den - dum est ma - gis so - li Ma - ri - ae ve - ra - ci
7. Sci - mus Chri - stum sur - re - xis - se a mor - tu - is ve - re:

quam Ju - dae - o - rum tur - bae fal - la - ci.]
tu no - bis, vi - ctor Rex, mi - se - re - re. A - men. Al - le - lu - ia.

LU, p. 780. Reprinted from Richard Hoppin, *Anthology of Medieval Music* (New York, 1978), No. 12, p. 15.

1. Victimae paschali laudes immolent Christiani.
2. Agnus redemit oves: Christus innocens Patri reconciliavit peccatores.

1. To the Paschal Victim let Christians offer songs of praise.
2. The Lamb has redeemed the sheep. Sinless Christ has reconciled sinners to the Father.

3. Mors et vita duelo conflixere mirando: dux vitae mortuus, regnat vivus.

4. Dic nobis Maria, quid vidisti in via? Sepulcrum Christi viventis, et gloriam vidi resurgentis:

5. Angelicos testes, sudarium, et vestes. Surrexit Christus spes mea: praecedet suos in Galilaeam.

6. Credendum est magis soli Mariae veraci quam Judaeorum turbae fallaci.

7. Scimus Christum surrexisse a mortuis vere: tu nobis, victor Rex, miserere.

WIPO OF BURGUNDY (d. 1048?)

3. Death and life have engaged in miraculous combat. The leader of life is slain, (yet) living he reigns.

4. Tell us, Mary, what you saw on the way? I saw the sepulchre of the living Christ and the glory of His rising;

5. The angelic witnesses, the shroud and vesture. Christ my hope is risen. He will go before his own into Galilee.

6. The truthful Mary alone is more to be believed than the deceitful crowd of Jews.

7. We know that Christ has truly risen from the dead. Thou conqueror and king, have mercy on us.

R. HOPPIN

Trope (dramatic dialogue):
Quem quaeritis in praesepe (10th century)
In die natale Domini stacio ad Sanctum Petrum

Incipiunt tropus [i.e. tropum] antequam dicatur officium

Respondent

Al -le -lu – ia, al – le -lu- ia! Iam ve -re sci – mus Chri-stus na – – tum in ter- ris, de quo

ca - ni -te o - mnes cum pro - phe - ta di – cen-tes, PU – ER NA – TUS EST NO – BIS.

(Introit of Third Mass)

In die natale Domini stacio ad Sanctum Petrum

Incipiunt tropus [i.e. tropum] antequam dicatur officium

Quem quaeritis in praesepe,
pastores, dicite?

Respondent
Salvatorem, Christum Dominum,
infantem pannis involutum,
secundum sermonem angelicum.

Respondent
Adest hic parvulus cum Maria,
matre sua, de qua dudum
vaticinando Isaias dixerat propheta:
Ecce virgo concipiet et
pariet filium; et nun euntes
dicite quia natus est.

Respondent
Alleluia, alleluia!
Iam vere scimus Christu natum
in terris, de quo canite omnes
cum propheta dicentes,
PUER NATUS EST NOBIS.

On the day of the nativity of the Lord, at the station of St. Peter

They begin the trope before the office [i.e. Introit] is said

Whom do you seek in the manger,
shepherds, please say?

Our savior, Christ the Lord,
an infant wrapped in cloths,
according to the angelic report.

The infant is attended here by Mary,
his mother, about whom a little while
ago the prophet Isiah foretold:
behold a virgin will conceive and
give birth to a son; and now as you go
tell that he is born.

Alleluia, alleluia!
Now truly we know that Christ was born
on earth, concerning which sing always
with the prophet, saying:
A SON IS BORN UNTO US.
(Introit of the Third Mass follows.)

The rubrics indicate that this dramatic dialogue was performed before the singing of the Introit at the Third Mass of Christmas Day at the altar which symbolized the Church of Saint Peter.

7

BERNART DE VENTADORN (CA. 1150–CA. 1180)

Can vei la lauzeta mover

1. Can vei la lau - ze - ta mo - ver De joi sas a - las con - tral rai,

Que s'o - blid' e·s_ lais - sa cha - zer___ Per la dous-sor_____ c'al cor li vai,___

Ai! tans grans en - vey - a m'en_____ ve De cui qu'eu vey - a jau - zi - on,

Me - ra - vil - has_____ ai, car des - se_____ Lo cor de de - zi - rer__ no·m fon.___

The dot between two parts of a word indicates a contraction. Hendrik Van der Werf, *The Chansons of the Troubadours and Trouvères* (Utrecht, 1972), pp. 91–93.

Can vei la lauzeta mover	When I see the lark beating
de joi sas alas contral rai,	its wings joyfully against the sun's rays,
que s'oblid' e·s laissa chazer	which then swoons and swoops down
per la doussor c'al cor li vai,	because of the joy in its heart,
ai! tan grans enveya m'en ve	oh! I feel such jealousy
de cui qu'eu veya jauzion,	for all those who have the joy of love,
meravilhas ai, car desse	that I am astonished
lo cor de dezirer no·m fon.	that my heart does not immediately melt with desire!
Ai, las! tan cuidava saber	Alas! I thought I knew so much
d'amor, e tan petit en sai,	of love, and I know so little;
car eu d'amar no·m posc tener	for I cannot help loving a lady
celeis don ja pro non aurai.	from whom I shall never obtain any favor.
Tout m'a mo cor, e tout m'a me,	She has taken away my heart and myself,
e se mezeis e tot lo mon;	and herself and the whole world;
e can se·m tolc, no·m laisset re	and when she left me, I had nothing left
mas dezirer e cor volon.	but desire and a yearning heart.
Anc non agui de me poder	I have no power over myself,
ni no fui meus de l'or' en sai	and have not had possession of myself
que·m laisset en sos olhs vezer	since the time when she allowed me to look into her eyes,
en un miralh que mout me plai.	in a mirror which I like very much.
Mirahls, pus me mirei en te,	Mirror, since I was reflected in you,
m'an mort li sospir depreon,	deep sighs have killed me,

c'aissi·m perdei com perdet se
lo bels Narcisus en la fon.

De las domnas me dezesper;
ja mais en lor no·m fiarai;
c'aissi com las solh chaptener,
enaissi las deschaptenrai.
Pois vei c'una pro no m'en te
vas leis que·m destrui e·m confon,
totas las dopt' e las mescre,
car be sai c'atretals se son.

D'aisso's fa be femna parer
ma domna, par qu'e·lh o retrai,
car no vol so c'om deu voler,

e so c'om li devada, fai.
Chazutz sui en mala merce,
et ai be faih co·l fols en pon;
e no sai per que m'esdeve,

mas car trop puyei contra mon.

Merces es perduda, per ver,
et eu non o saubi anc mai,
car cilh qui plus en degr'aver
no·n a ges, et on la querrai?
A! can mal sembla, qui la ve,

qued aquest chaitiu deziron

que ja ses leis non aura be,
laisse morir, que no l'aon!

Pus ab midons no·m pot valer
precs ni merces ni·l dreihz qu'eu ai,
ni a leis no ven a plazer
qu'eu l'am, ja mais no·lh o dirai.

Aissi·m part de leis e·m recre;
mort m'a, e per mort h respon,
e van m'en, pus ilh no·m rete,

chaitius, en issilh, no sai on.

Tristans, ges no·n auretz de me,
qu'eu m'en vau, chaitius, no sai on.

De chantar me gic e·m recre,
e de joi d'amor m'escon.

for I caused my own ruin, just as
fair Narcissus caused his by looking in the
fountain.

I despair of ladies;
I shall not trust them ever again;
just as I used to defend them,
now I shall condemn them.
Since I see that *one* of them does not help me
against her who is ruining and destroying me
I fear them all and have no faith in them,
for I know they are all the same.

My lady shows herself to be [merely] a woman
(and that is why I reproach her)
in that she does not want what one should
want,
and she does what is forbidden her.
I have fallen out of favor,
and have acted like the fool on the bridge;
and I do not know why this has happened to
me,
unless it was because I tried to climb too high.

Mercy is gone, that is sure,
and I never received any of it,
for she who should have the most mercy
has none, and where else should I seek it?
Oh! how difficult it is for a person who sees
her
to imagine that she would allow to die this
poor yearning wretch,
and would not help the man
who can have no help but her!

Since pleas and mercy and my rights
cannot help me to win my lady,
and since it does not please her
that I love her, I shall speak to her about it no
more.
So I am leaving her and her service;
she has killed me, and I reply with death,
and I am going sadly away, since she will not
accept
my service, into exile, I do not know where.

Tristan, you will hear no more of me,
for I am going sadly away, I do not know
where,
I am going to stop singing,
and I flee from love and joy.

COMTESSA [BEATRIZ] DE DIA (D. CA. 1212)
Canso: *A chantar* (second half, 12th century)

Transcribed by Hendrik van der Werf in The Extant Troubadour Melodies (Rochester: Author, 1984), p. 13. Gerald A. Bond, text editor. Used by permission.

To sing I must of what I'd rather not,
so much does he of whom I am the lover embitter me;
yet I love him more than anything in the world.

To no avail are my beauty, my politeness,
my goodness, or my virtue and good sense.
For I have been cheated and betrayed,
as if I had been disagreeable to him.

(The genders of the speaker and beloved are inconsistent in this version of the text, as in the second line the subject, "cele" (she), is feminine and the speaker, "amigs" (lover), is masculine, whereas in the last line the subject, "lui" (him), is masculine. In another version "cele" is "de lui," and "amigs" is "amia," which fits the music better. The remaining four stanzas have been omitted.)

ADAM DE LA HALLE (CA. 1237–CA. 1287)
Jeu de Robins et de Marion:
Rondeau, *Robins m' aime*

Friedrich Gennrich, *Troubadours, Trouvères, Minne – und Meistergesang* (Cologne, 1951), p. 38.

Robin m'aime,	Robin loves me,
Robin m'a,	Robin has me,
Robins m'a demandée	Robin asked me
Si m'ara.	if he can have me.
Robins m'acata cotele	Robin took off my skirt
D'escarlate bonnet et belle,	of scarlet, good and pretty,
Souskanie et chainturele.	my bodice and girdle.
Aleuriva!	Hurray!

WIZLAU VON RÜGEN (CA. 1268–1325)

We *ich han gedacht*

Transcribed from the neumatic notation in Georg Holz, Franz Saran and Eduard Bernouilli, *Die Jenaer Liederhandschrift* (Leipzig, 1901), I, 130.

Alas, I have been thinking
this whole night
of my great burdens,
which a woman begot
and which do not allow me
to feel at all secure
that she might want to approach me:
a little kiss
from her mouth is a lovely thing,
which I would gladly accept.

Such a sweet creature,
with all your fine breeding:
yet you want to destroy me?
On him who seeks affection
and hopes for it from you
you ought to bestow happiness.
This would be my advice:
that you give love's pledge
in his hand
from your heart's midst.

Whatever I sang,
I never rose
to your noble love:
therefore I suffer distress,
a stray death,
which I thereby achieve.
Always will I come begging to you.
No advice will help me,
as I now feel
in my heart's midst.

II

HANS SACHS (1494–1576)
Nachdem David war redlich und aufrichtig

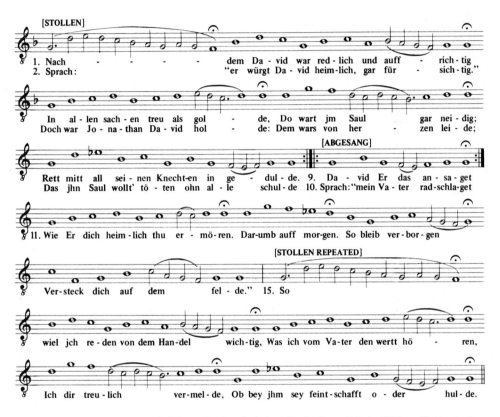

[STOLLEN]

1. Nach — dem Da - vid war red - lich und auff - rich - tig
2. Sprach: "er würgt Da - vid heim - lich, gar für - sich - tig."

In al - len sach - en treu als gol - de, Do wart jm Saul gar nei - dig;
Doch war Jo - na - than Da - vid hol - de: Dem wars von her - zen lei - de;

[ABGESANG]

Rett mitt all sei - nen Knecht-en in ge - dul - de. 9. Da - vid Er das an - sa - get
Das jhn Saul wollt' tö - ten ohn al - le schul - de 10. Sprach: "mein Va - ter rad-schla-get

11. Wie Er dich heim - lich thu er - mö - ren. Dar - umb auff mor - gen. So bleib ver - bor - gen

[STOLLEN REPEATED]

Ver - steck dich auf dem fel - de." 15. So

wiel jch re - den von dem Han-del wich-tig, Was ich vom Va-ter den wertt hö - ren,

Ich dir treu - lich ver - mel - de, Ob bey jhm sey feint-schafft o - der hul - de.

Adapted from diplomatic copy in G. Münzer, *Das Singebuch des Adam Puschman* (Leipzig, 1906), p. 80. Notation in whole and half notes, some with dots, is in the original manuscript in Wroclaw, Municipal Library. Half-notes are meant to go much faster than whole notes. Dotted half-notes are somewhat prolonged. Puschman labels this *Weise* or melodic formula "Klingende Ton" (chiming or ringing mode).

Nachdem David war redlich und aufrichtig,	Since David was honest and candid,
In allen sachen treu als golde,	in all things true as gold,
Do wart jm Saul gar neidig;	so Saul was very jealous of him.
Rett mit all seinen knechten in gedulde.	He dealt with all his vassals with patience.
Sprach: "er würgt David heimlich, gar fürsichtig."	Said he: "He struggled with David secretly, cautiously.
Doch war Jonathan David holde;	Yet Jonathan was kind to David;
Dem wars von herzen leide,	it was painful to his heart

39

Das jhn Saul wollte töten ohn alle schulde.

David Er das ansaget,
Sprach: "mein Vater radschlaget,
Wie Er dich heimlich thu ermören.
Darumb auff morgen,
So bleib verborgen,
Versteck dich auf dem felde."
So wiel ich reden von dem handel wichtig,
Was ich vom Vater den wertt hören,
Ich dir treu vermelde,
Ob bey ihm sey feintschaft oder hulde.

that Saul wanted to kill him [David] without
    any blame.
Thus he spoke to David:
saying, "My father turned a somersault,
when he secretly [planned] to murder you;
therefore in the morning
remain concealed,
hide yourself in the field."
As much as I tell of the affair is important;
what I, concerning the father's honor, heard,
I truthfully impart,
whether there was hostility in him or kindness.

Istampita Palamento

Jan ten Bokum, *De Dansen* (Utrecht, 1976), pp. 49–50. Facsimile in Gilbert Reaney ed., *The Manuscript London, British Museum, Additional 29987* (American Institute of Musicology, 1965), fols. 60r–61v.

Quinta pars.

Organum: *Tu patris sempiternus es filius*
(ca. 900)

a) *Tu patris sempiternus es filius* (two voices)

[Vox principalis]
[Vox organalis]

Tu pa - tris sem - pi - ter - nus es   fi - li - us.

b) *Tu patris sempiternus es filius* (four voices)

Vox organalis

Tu pa - tris sem - pi - ter - nus es   fi - li - us.

Vox principalis
Vox organalis
Vox principalis

c) *Te humiles famuli modulis venerando piis* (two voices)

Vox principalis

Vox organalis

Te   hu - mi - les fa - mu - li mo - du - lis ve - ne - ran - do pi - is.
Se   iu - be - as fla - gi - tant va - ri - is li - be - ra - re ma - lis.

From Anonymous, *Musica enchiriadis*, chs. 13–14, 18, ed. Hans Schmid, *Musica et Scolica Enchiriadis* (Munich: Bayerischen Akademie der Wissenschaften, 1981), pp. 38–39, transcribed in *Musica Enchiriadis* and *Scolica Enchiriadis,* tr. Raymond Erickson, ed. Claude V. Palisca (New Haven: Yale University Press, forthcoming).

Tu patris sempiternus es filius.

Te humiles famuli modulis
    venerando piis,
se iubeas flagitant variis
    liberare malis.

You, of the father are the everlasting son.

[Your] humble servants,
    worshipping with pious melodies,
beseech you, as you command, to free
    them from diverse ills.

 14

Organum: *Alleluia Justus ut palma*
(ca. 1100)

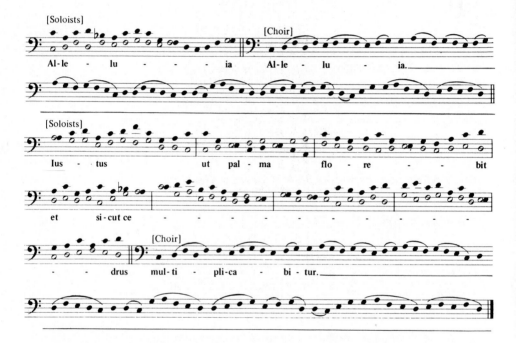

Milan, Biblioteca Ambrosiana, MS M.17 sup., ed. Hans Heinrich Eggebrecht and Frieder Zaminer, *Ad organum facien-dum, Lehrschriften der Mehrstimmigkeit in nachguidonischer Zeit* (Mainz, 1970), p. 53.

Alleluia Justus ut palma florebit,
et sicut cedrus multiplicabitur.

Alleluia. The righteous shall flourish
like a palm tree and shall multiply like a cedar.

15

Versus: *Senescente mundano filio*

Se - ne - scen - te mun - da - no fi - li - o /

Quem fo-ve-bat men - tis o - bli - vi -

o / Ve - nit spon-sus di - vi-na ra - ti - - o /

Co - mes e - ius est re-stau - ra - ci -

- o / So - la vir - go re -

ga - lis fi - li - a / Di - gna di - gnis pa-rat hos-pi - ci - a /

Transcribed by Sarah Ann Fuller from Paris, Bibliothèque Nationale, MS lat. 3549, fol. 153.
(♪) denotes no fixed durational value. Notes flagged together belong to the same ligature. (♪) is a plica, and (/) indicates the end of a poetic line. Notes in brackets have been supplied.

Ap-ta co -mes   re-plet pa-la-ti - a / Au-lam   spon-sus

in - trat   per ho - sti -   a.

Senescente mundano filio	While the earthly son grows old
Quem fovebat mentis oblivio	whom forgetfulness was favoring,
Venit sponsus divina ratio	comes the bridegroom, divine reason.
Comes eius est restauracio.	His companion is refreshment.
Sola virgo regalis filia	Sole virgin, royal daughter,
Digna dignis para hospitia	prepare guest chambers worthy of the deserving;
Apta comes replet palacia	a fitting companion fills the palaces.
Aulam sponsus intrat per hostia.	The bridegroom enters the hall through the doors.

16

Alleluia Pascha nostrum

Gregorian chant and early polyphony based on it

a) *Alleluia Pascha nostrum*, Plainchant

Gordon A. Anderson, *The Latin Compositions in Fascicules VII and VIII of the Notre Dame Manuscript Wolfenbüttel Helmstadt 1099*, Part II, p. 276. Réproduit avec permission de l'Institut de musique médiévale, Henryville, Ottawa et Binningen.

b) Léonin (fl. 1160–80), Organum duplum, *Alleluia Pascha nostrum*

Florence, Biblioteca Medicea-Laurenziana, MS pluteus 29.1, fol. 109; the clausulae are from Anderson, II, 25–26.

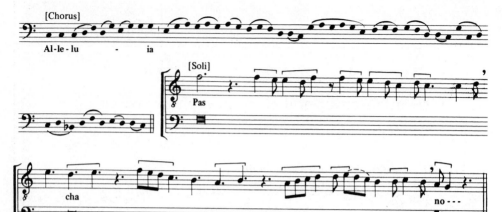

[Chorus]

Al - le - lu - ia

[Soli]

Pas

cha

no - - -

Duplum

Cantus

No - - strum.

(continued on p. 52)

c) Conductus-motet on Léonin's clausula on *nostrum*

Triplum / Duplum / Cantus

Gau - de - at de - vo - ti - o fi - de - li - um; Ver - bum pa - tris in - car - na - tur,

Nostrum.

No - va pro - les no - bis da - tur Et no - bis - cum con - ver - sa - tur Sa - lus gen - ti - um. Vi - te pan - dit

o - sti - um, Dum mor - tis sup - pli - ci - um, Pi - e to - le - rat. Mun - di prin - ceps ex - tur - ba - tur,

Dum con - si - de - rat, Quod per mor - tem li - be - ra - tur Qui per - i - e - rat, Iu - re su - o

sic pri - va - tur, Dum de - si - de - rat Il - lum si - bi sub - de - re, qui nil com - mi - se - rat.

Anderson, II, 25–26.

d) Substitute clausula on *nostrum*

Florence, MS pluteus 29.1, fol. 157v, ed. Anderson, II, 199–200.

e) Motet, *Salve, salus hominum—O radians stella—nostrum*

Triplum
Sal - ve, sa - lus ho - mi - num, Spes mi-se - ri - cor-di - e,

Duplum
O ra - di - ans stel-la pre ce-te - ris, Sum - mi De - i ma-ter

Cantus
Nostrum.

Spes ve-ni - e, Pur-ga - trix cri-mi - num, Ce - cis lu - men lu - mi - num,

et fi - li - a, E - xi-mi - a pro-les de - ge - ne - ris, Tu ge-ne -

Ma - ter, pru - den-ti - e, Si - gnum vi - e, Ter-mi - nus pa-tri -

ris Mun-di le - ti - ti - a, Tu de vi - a tri-bu - los con-te - ris,

e, Spes ve-ni - e, Nec-tar, flos glo-ri - e, Iu - sti - ti - e Sol pi -

Spes mi-se - ris, Ho-mi - nis Ne - sci - a, Ma-ri - a, De la - te - ris lu - to

e, Cle - men-ti - e So-bri - e Ros, vir-go mun-di-ti - e.

nos li-be - ra, Re - ge-ne - rans ge-nus in po-ste - ris re-gi - a.

Anderson, II, 199–200.

b) Léonin, Organum duplum, *Alleluia Pascha nostrum* (continued)

(continued on p. 54)

f) Motet, *Ave Maria, Fons letitie—latus* on Léonin's clausula on *latus*

Anderson, II, 73–76.

b) Léonin, Organum duplum, *Alleluia Pascha nostrum* (continued)

g) Motet, *Qui d' amors veut bien—Qui longuement porroit—nostrum* on substitute clausula on *nostrum* (16d)

Hans Tischler, *The Earliest Motets,* Yale University Press, Motet 137–1. Printed by permission.

a) Alleluia. Pascha nostrum immolatus est Christus.

Alleluia. Christ, our paschal lamb, is sacrified.

c) Gaudeat devotio fidelium;
Verbum patris incarnatur,
Nova proles nobis datur
Et nobis cum conversatur
Salus gentium.
Vite pandit ostium,
Dum mortis supplicium,
Pie tolerat.
Mundi princeps exturbatur,
Dum considerat,
Quod per morten liberatur
Qui perierat.
Iure suo sic privatur,
Dum desiderat
Illum sibi subdere, qui nihil commiserat.

Let the devotion of the faithful be raised in rejoicing;
the word of the father is made flesh,
and a new child is given to us,
and He has bestowed Himself upon us.
The salvation of the people
has opened the gateway of life,
for he in devotion has borne
the punishment of death.
Satan was cast down
when He stood firm
so that through His death
he who had perished might be made free;
thus was He stripped of His own divine nature
when He, unflinching,
chose to subdue death unto Himself—He who had committed no sin.

Triplum

e) Salve, salus hominum,
Spes misericordie,
Spes venie,
Purgatric criminum,
Cecis lumen luminum,
Mater prudentie,
Signum vie,
Terminus patrie,
Spes venie,
Nectar, flos glorie,
Iustitie
Sol pie,
Clementie
Sobrie
Ros, virgo munditie.

Hail, safety of men,
hope of pity,
hope of pardon,
cleanser of sins,
light of light to the blind,
Mother of prudence,
sign-post of the way,
boundary of Heaven,
hope of pardon,
nectar, flower of glory,
of justice,
holy sun,
of temperate
Purgatrix
dew, Virgin of cleanliness!

Adapted from ANDERSON, II, 324.

Duplum

O radians stella pre ceteris,
Summi Dei mater et filia,
Eximia proles degeneris,
Tu generis Mundi letitia,
Tu de via tribulos conteris,
Spes miseris,
Hominis
Nescia Maria
De lateris luto nos libera,
Regenerans genus in posteris regia.

O shining star, outshining all others,
Mother and Daughter of the highest God,
peerless offspring of a degenerate race,
Thou art the joy of the people of the world.
Thou turnest away the perils of the way.
O hope of wretched
Man;
Mary, not knowing [the touch of man],
free us from the mire surrounding us,
regenerating the human race THY KINGDOM FOR ALL AGES.

f) Ave Maria,
  Fons letitie,
  Virgo pura, pia,
  Vas munditie,
  Te voce varia
  Sonet sobrie
  Gens leta sobria.
  Gaudens varie
  Promat ecclesia
  Laudes Marie,
  Vox ecclesie.
  Sonet in maria.
  Hec solvit scrinia
  Ysaie,
  Reserans ostia
  Clausa patrie,
  Via dans eximia
  Regem glorie,
  Qui sola gratia,
  Plenus gratie,
  Factus est hostia,
  Finis hostie.

Hail Mary,
fount of Joy,
virgin pure and holy,
vessel of chastity,
may the joyous people
sing Thee in various
yet restrained voices.
Rejoicing for many blessings,
let the Church express
its praise for Mary;
and let the voice of the Church
resound in the sea.
She has fulfilled the prophecies
of Isaiah,
unlocking the once-closed
gates of heaven,
granting access by a wonderful way
to the King of Glory,
who by grace alone,
and full of grace,
was made sacrifice,
the end of all sacrifice.

ANDERSON, II, 52–53

Triplum

g) Qui d'amors veut bien joir
  Et gueredon en atent,
  Ne la doit pas longuement maintenir.
  Qui la maintient longuement,
  Por tant que repentir
  A son voloir ne s'en puet maintenant;
  Lors l'en doit bien celui por fol tenir;
  Car on voit bien avenir,
  Que cil qui meins i atent
  Plus i recuevre souvent.

He who wishes to enjoy love
and awaits its reward
must not for a long time
keep waiting;
he who does so for a long time
has not now the opportunity
to repent for his excesses.
One can scarcely consider him a fool for it,
for it is easy to see in the future
that he who least expects it
will regain it most often.

Duplum

Qui longuement porroit joir d'amors,
Il n'est deduit, qui mieuz vausist d'amer;

Mais l'en i a souvent larmes et plors,
Et quant en i cuide joie trover,
Lors n'i trove ne solas ne secors,
Qui amors veut sans faintise esprover,

A tous jors
Face semblant, qu'au cuer n'en ait doulor;

Si en porra joir et recouvrer
Les douçors.

He who would enjoy love for a long time,
hath no pleasure which is more worthwhile
    than love;
but there are often tears and crying in it,
And when one thinks of finding joy in it,
then one finds no solace or help.
He who wants to experience love without de-
    ceit,
For ever
Let him pretend that he has no grief in his
    heart:
And he will be able to enjoy and regain the
    sweetness of it.

Adapted from ANDERSON, II, 324–25.

PÉROTIN (CA. 1183–CA. 1238)
Organum quadruplum: *Sederunt*
Gradual for St. Stephen's Day, Respond only

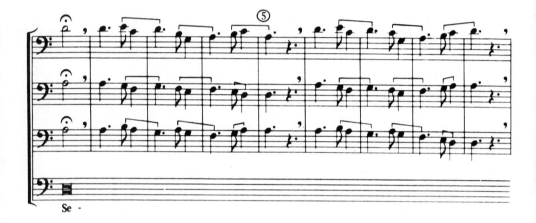

Reprinted from Hoppin, *AMM* No. 35, pp. 59–66.

de -

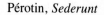

runt.

Chorus

prin - ci - pes,   et ad - ver-sum me   lo - que - ban - tur:

et in - i - qui per-se - cu - ti   sunt   me.

The rulers were seated in council, and they spoke against me; and my enemies persecuted me.

R. HOPPIN

18

Conductus: *Ave virgo virginum*
(13th century)

Florence, Biblioteca Laurenziana, MS Pluteus 29.1, fol. 240r–240v.

Ave virgo virginum
Verbi carnis cella,
In salutem hominum
Stillans lac et mella.
Peperisti dominum,
Moysi ficella,
O radio
Sol exit, et luminum
Fontem parit stella.

Ave, plena gratia,
Caput Zabulonis
Contrivisti spolia
Reparans predonis.
Celi rorans pluvia
Vellus Gedeonis,
O filio
Tu nos reconcilia,
Mater Salomonis.

Virgo tu mosayce
Rubus visionis,
De te fluxit sylice
Fons redemptionis.
Quos redemit calice
Christus passionis,
O gaudio
Induat glorifice
Resurrectionis

Hail, virgin of virgins,
shrine of the word made flesh,
who for man's salvation
drips milk and honey.
You bore the Lord;
you were a rush-basket for Moses;
O, from your rays
the sun goes forth, and the star
brings forth a fountain of light.

Hail, full of grace,
chief of Zebulun,
the spoils of robbers
you restore.
Like rain, falling from heaven
on the fleece of Gideon,
with your son
reunite us,
O mother of Solomon!

You, Virgin,
bramble-bush of the Mosaic vision,
from you flowed the fountain
through the rock of redemption.
Those Christ has redeemed through the chalice
of his passion,
O, may he clothe them with the joy
of his glorious
resurrection.

19

Motet: *Aucun vont—Amor qui cor—Kyrie*
(late 13th century)

1) Kyrie eleison*

Reprinted from Hoppin, *AMM* No. 54, pp. 112–15.

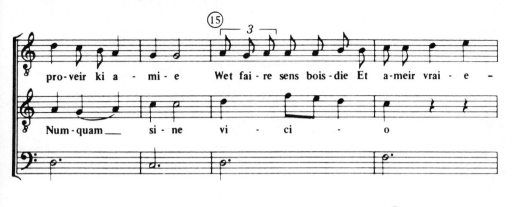

pro - veir ki a - mi - e Wet fai - re sens bois - die Et a - meir vrai - e -

Num - quam ___ si - ne vi - ci - o

ment, Car ja en li n'iert as - si - se Vi - lo - ni - e Ne con - voi - ti -

Vel ra - ro pot - est es - se,

se D'a - mas - seir ar - gent, Ains ai - me bu - ne com - pa - gnie Et des -

Quo - ni - am est ne - ces - se

2)

pent a - des lar - ge - ment, Et si n'at en li fe - lo - ni - e N'en - vi - e Sor au - tre

Ex quo ___ plus di - li - gi - tur

Triplum

Aucun vont sovent	Some, through envy,
Por lor envie	often speak
Mesdisant d'amur,	ill of love;
Mais ilh n'est si bone vie	But there is no life so good
Com d'amer loiaument;	as loving loyally.
Car d'ameir vient tote cortoisie,	For from loving comes all courtesy,
Tote honur	all honor,
Et tos biens ensengnemens.	and all good breeding.
Tot ce puet en li proveir ki amie	All this can one experience

Wet faire sens boisdie
Et ameir vraiement,
Car ja en li n'iert assise
Vilonie Ne convoitise
D'amasseir argent,
Ains aime bune compagnie
Et despent ades largement,
Et si n'at en li felonie
N'envie
Sor autre gent.

Mais ver chascun s'umilie
Et parolle cortoisement
S'ilh at dou tot, sens partie,
Mis sun cuer en ameir entierement.
Et sachies k'ilh n'aime mie,
Ains ment,
Si silh soi demainne autrement.

who wishes without falseness to have
a lover and to love truly;
for never in him will there be
villany or covetousness
to amass money.
But he loves good company
and spends freely;
and in him is no treachery
nor envy
of others.

But he is humble to all
and speaks courteously,
if he has wholly, without division,
given his heart entirely to loving.
And you may know that he loves not at all,
but lies,
if he conducts himself otherwise.

Duplum

Amor qui cor vulnerat
Humanum, quem generat
Carnalis affectio,
Numquam sine vicio
Vel raro potest esse,
Quoniam est necesse
Ex quo plus diligitur
Res que cito labitur
Vel transit, eo minus
Diligatur Dominus.

Love that wounds
the human heart,
that carnal affection generates,
can never or rarely,
be without vice,
since necessarily,
the more a thing that
quicky escapes or passes
is loved, the less
the Lord is loved.

R. HOPPIN

20

Motet: *Pucelete—Je languis—Domino*
(late 13th century)

- mant. 10. N'est en mai 11. ain - si gai 12. ros -

4. trop est jo - - - -

- si - gno - let chan - tant. 13. S'a - me - rai 14. de cuer en - tie - re -

- li - - e la _____ mort.

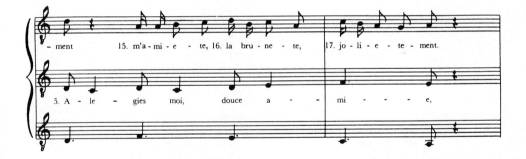

- ment 15. m'a - mi - e - te, 16. la bru - ne - te, 17. jo - li - e - te - ment.

5. A - le - gies moi, douce a - mi - - - e,

18. Bele a - mi - e, 19. qui ma vie 20. en vo bail - lie 21. a - ves te - nu - e ___

6. ce - ste ma - la - - di - - - e,

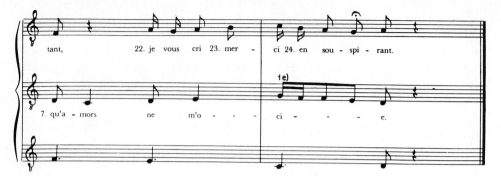

tant,   22. je vous cri 23. mer - ci 24. en sou - spi - rant.

1e)

7. qu'a - mors   ne   m'o - - - ci - - - - e.

Pucelete	Fair maiden,
bele et avenant,	lovely and comely;
joliete,	pretty maiden,
polie et plesant	courteous and pleasing,
la sadete	delicious one,
que je desir tant,	whom I desire so much
mi fait lies,	you make me merry,
jolis, envoisies	neat, friendly,
et amant.	and loving.
N'est en mai	In May there is no
ainsi gai	such happy
rossignolet chantant.	nightingale singing.
S'amerai	I shall love
de cuer entierement	with all my heart
m'amiete,	my sweetheart,
la brunete,	the brunette,
jolietement.	very happily.
Bele amie,	Sweet friend,
qui ma vie	who my life
en vo baillie	have held in ransom
avest tenue tant,	for so long,
je vous cri	I appeal to you
merci	for pity,
en souspirant.	sighing.

Je langui des maus d'amors:	I languish from love-sickness:
Miez aim assez, qu'il m'ocie	I would rather that it kill me
que nul autre maus;	than any other illness;
trop est jolie la mort.	such a death is too beautiful.
Alegies moi, douce amie,	Relieve me, sweet friend,
ceste maladie,	of this malady,
qu'amors ne m'ocie.	lest love kill me.

21

Philippe de Vitry (1291–1361)
Motet from *Roman de Fauvel:*
Garrit Gallus—In nova fert—Neuma

Reprinted from Hoppin, *AMM* No. 59, pp. 120–26.

A2. 1

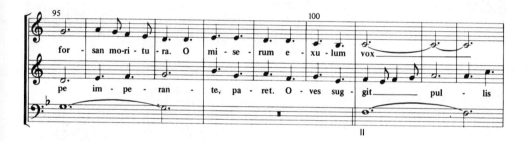

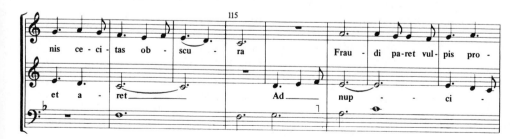

Triplum

The cock babbles, lamenting sorrowfully,
for the whole assembly of cocks*
mourns because, while serving vigilantly,
it is trickily betrayed by the satrap.
And the fox,† like a grave robber,
thriving with the astuteness of Belial,
rules as a monarch with the consent
of the lion himself.‡ Ah, what slavery!
Lo, once again Jacob's family
is exiled by another Pharaoh.
Not, as formerly, able to escape
to the homeland of Judah, they weep.
Stricken by hunger in the desert,
lacking the help of arms,
although they cry out, they are robbed;
perhaps speedily they will die.
O harsh voice of the wretched exiles;
O sorrowfully babbling of the cocks,
since the dark blindness of the lion
submits to the fraud of the traitorous fox.
You who suffer the arrogance of his misdeeds,
rise up,
or what you have of honor is being or
will be lost, because if avengers are slow
men soon turn to evil doing.

* Gallus: cock; or Gauls (the French)

† Enguerran de Marigny, chief councillor of the French king

‡ Philip IV the Fair

Duplum

My heart is set upon speaking of forms
changed into new (bodies).§
The evil dragon that renowned Michael once
utterly defeated by the miraculous power
of the Cross,
now endowed with the grace of Absalom,
now with the cheerful eloquence of Ulysses,
now armed with wolfish teetch
a soldier in the service of Thersites,
lives again changed into a fox
whose tail the lion deprived
of sight obeys, while the fox reigns.
He sucks the blood of sheep and is satiated
with chickens.
Alas, he does not cease sucking and still
thirsts;
he does not abstain from meats at the wedding
feast.
Woe now to the chickens, woe to the blind
lion.
In the presence of Christ, finally, woe to
the dragon.

R. HOPPIN

§ Ovid *Metamorphoses*, 1,1.

22

Jacopo da Bologna (14th century)
Madrigal: Fenice fù

Nino Pirrotta, ed. *The Collected Works of Jacobo da Bologna and Vincenzo da Rimini* (American Institute of Musicology, 1963), p. 6. Reprinted by permission of A. Carapetyan, Director and Hänssler-Verlag, West Germany. All rights reserved. International copyright secured.

Fenice fù e vissi pura e morbida,   A phoenix was I who lived pure and tender
Et or son trasmutat' in una tortora,   and now am transformed into a turtle-dove
Che vollo con amor per le belle ortora   that flies with love through the beautiful or-
                                                   chards, [and]
Arbor[e] secho [mai] n'aqua torbida,   the dry woods [but] never in muddy waters.
No' me deleta may per questo dubito,   It gives me no pleasure because of this doubt.
Va ne l'astate l'inverno vende subito.   Go in the summer; winter comes quickly.
Tal vissi e tal me vivo e posso scrivere   So I lived and so I live and can write,
C'ha donna non è più chè honesta vivere.   which, for a woman, is no more than to live
                                                   honestly.

23

FRANCESCO LANDINI (CA. 1327–97)
Ballata: *Non avrà ma' pietà*

Leo Schrade, ed., *Polyphonic Music of the Fourteenth Century,* IV (Paris: Oiseau Lyre, 1958), 144–45. Used by permission of Hänssler-Verlag, W. Germany.

Non avrà ma' pietà questa mie donna.
Se tu non faj, amore,
Ch'ella sia certa del mio grande ardore.
S'ella sapesse quanta pena i' porto
Per onestà celata nella mente
Sol per la sua bellecça, che conforto
D'altro non prende l'anima dolente,
Forse da lej sarebbono in me spente
Le fiamme che la pare
Di giorno in giorno acrescono 'l dolore.

She will never have mercy, this lady of mine,
if you do not see to it, love,
that she is certain of my great ardor.
If she knew how much pain I bear—
for honesty's sake concealed in my mind—
only for her beauty, other than which
nothing gives comfort to a grieving soul,
perhaps by her would be extinguished in me
the flames which seem to arouse in
her from day to day more pain.

B. D'ALESSIO DONATI

24

GUILLAUME DE MACHAUT (CA. 1300–77)
Double Ballade: *Quant Theseus—Ne quier veoir*

Leo Schrade, ed., *The Works of Guillaume de Machaut,* in *Polyphonic Music of the Fourteenth Century,* III (Paris: Oiseau Lyre, 1956), 124–27. Reprinted by permission.

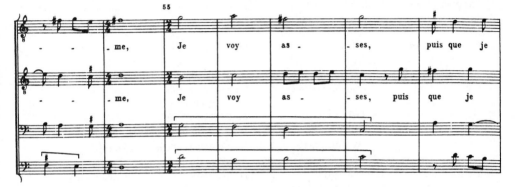

Quant Theseus, Hercules et Jason
Chercherent tout, et terre et mer parfonde,
Pour accroistre leur pris et leur renon
Et pour veoir bien tout l'estat dou monde,
Moult furent dignes d'onnour.
Mais quant je voy de biauté l'umble flour,
Assevis sui de tout, si que, par m'ame,
Je voy assés, puis que je voy ma dame.

Ne quier veoir la biauté d'Absalon
Ne de Ulixés le sens et la faconde,
Ne esprouver la force de Sanson,
Ne regarder que Dalila le tonde,
Ne cure n'ay par nul tour
Des yeus Argus ne de joie gringnour,
Car pour plaisance et sans aide d'ame,
Je voy assés, puis que je voy ma dame.

Car en veant sa biaute, sa façon
Et son maintiens qui de doucour seuronde
Je y preing assez bein pour devenir bon,
Car le grant bien de li en moy redonde
Par grace de fine amour
Qui me contraint a hayr deshonnour
Et tout vice; si puis dire sanz blasme:
Je voy assez, puis que je voy ma dame.

Veoir ne quier la doree toison
Ne les Yndes ne de Rouge Mer onde,
N'aus infernaus penre guerre, ou tencon
Pour eslongier le regart de la blonde
Dont me vient joye et baudour
Et doulz penser; si tieng pour le millous
Que, a tout conter et bien peser a drame,
Je voy assez, puis que je voy ma dame.
        THOMAS PAIEN

De l'ymage que fist Pymalion
Elle n'avoit pareille ne seconde;
Mais la belle qui m'a en sa prison
Cent mille fois est plus belle et plus monde:
C'est uns drois fluns de doucour
Qui puet et scet garir toute dolour;
Dont cilz a tort qui de dire me blame:
Je voy assez, puis que je voy ma dame.

Si ne me chaut dou sens de Salemon,

Ne que Phebus entermine, ou responde,
Ne que Venus s'en mesle ne Mennon
Que Jupiter fist muer en aronde,
Car je di, quant je l'aour,
Aym et desir, ser et drieng et honnous,
Et que s'amour seur tout rien m'enflame:
Je voy assez, puis que je voy ma dame.
        GUILLAUME DE MACHAUT

When Theseus, Hercules and Jason
sought everywhere over land and deep sea
to enhance their valor and reknown
and to view fully the state of the world,
they were most worthy of honor.
But when I see of beauty a humble flower,
I am entirely content, for upon my soul,
I see enough, when I behold my lady

I am not curious to see the beauty of Absalom
or Ulysses' wisdom and eloquence,
or try the strength of Samson,
or see Dalilah cut his locks.
I do not care at all
for Argus' eyes nor any rare joy,
because for my pleasure, and with no help
I see enough, when I behold my lady

For, in seeing her beauty, her countenance,
and her bearing, imbued with sweetness,
I acquire wealth enough to become rich,
for her great goodness redounds in me
by virtue of her noble love,
which compels me to hate dishonor
and all vice; so I can guilessly say:
I see enough, when I behold my lady.

I seek not to view the Golden Fleece,
nor the Indies, nor the Red Sea's waves.
I shall not take on infernal wars or battles
to stretch the distance from the blond
from whom come my joy, happiness,
and sweet thoughts; so I consider it best
that, when all is counted and weighed,
I see enough, when I behold my lady.

To the likeness that Pygmalion made
there was no equal nor second;
but the fair lady who has imprisoned me
is a thousand times fairer and purer.
She is truly a swift current of sweetness
who can and knows how to heal all pain;
those are wrong who charge I err when I say:
I see enough, when I behold my lady.

It concerns me not to lack the wisdom of
        Solomon,
nor that Phoebus intimate or respond,
nor that Venus intervene, nor even Meno,
whom Jupiter made revolve;
for I say how much I adore,
love, and desire her, serve and honor her,
and if love for her inflames me totally,
I see enough, when I behold my lady.

25

GUILLAUME DE MACHAUT
Mass: *Agnus Dei*

Edited by Elizabeth Keitel for "Early Musical Masterworks."

Ag- - - - nus de- - -
Ag- - - - - nus de- - -
Ag- - - nus de- -
Ag- - - - - - - nus de-

- - - i qui tol- - -
- - - i qui tol- - -
- - - i qui tol- -
- - - i qui tol- - - -

- lis pec- - - ca- - -
- lis pec- - ca- -
lis pec- - - ca- ta
lis pec- - - ca- ta

For translation of the text see p. 17.

Solage (late 14th century)
Rondeau: *Fumeux fume*

Willi Apel, ed. *French Secular Music of the Late Fourteenth Century,* (Mediaeval Academy of America, 1950), 64.
Reprinted by permission.

Fumeux fume par fumee
Fumeuse speculacion.
Qu'antre fummet sa pensee
Fumeux fume par fumee.

Quar fumer molt li agree
Tant qu'il ait son entencion.
Fumeux fume par fumee
Fumeuse speculacion.

Smoky fumes through smoke,
smoky speculation.
When another smokes his thoughts,
Smoky fumes through smoke.

For smoking certainly agrees with him,
as long as he gets what he wants.
Smoky fumes through smoke
smoky speculation.

27

Rondellus motet from Worcester:
Fulget coelestis curia

Luther Dittmer, *The Worcester Fragments* (American Institute of Musicology, 1957), pp. 49–50. Reprinted by permission of A. Carapetyan, Director and Hänssler-Verlag, West Germany. All rights reserved. International copyright secured.

Tenor 1

Fulget coelestis curia
Petro sedente praeside
Sub poli principe:
Roma gaudet de tali praesule
Dato divino munere
Plaudat orbis cum gloria
Petro pri[vilegia
Portante] cuncta a mortali criminae.
Solvendi sordida,
Petre tu nobis respice
Ea nobis deice
Quae sunt obnoxia.

Heaven's court shines forth,
with Peter sitting as guard
under the Prince of Heaven.
Rome delights in such a bishop,
granted by divine gift.
Let the earth resound with glory,
while Peter delivers the privileged
from mortal sin.
Absolving sin,
Peter, have regard for us:
cast away from us those things
that are reprehensible.

Tenor 2

O Petre flos apostolorum
Pastor coelestis curiae,
Oves pasce melliflue;
Ducens ad supera
Nostra corda fove laetitia;
Praebe praesidia.
Nostrorum scelerum tolle malitiam
A summo principe
Nobis implora veniam
Nos deduc ad summa guadia.

O Peter, flower of the apostles,
shepherd of the heavenly court,
nourish your sheep sweetly,
leading them to higher things.
Our hearts, warm up with gladness;
grant us protection.
Bear the iniquity of our evil deeds.
From the highest prince
beg for us mercy;
lead us away to supreme joys.

Tenor 3

Roma gaudet de tali praesule
Dato divino munere.
Fulget coeslestis curia
Petro sedente praeside
Sub poli principe.
Solvendi crimina
Praebe praesidia.
Plaudat orbis cum gloria
Petro privilegia
Portante cuncta a mortali crimine.

Rome delights in such a bishop,
granted by divine gift.
Heaven's court shines forth,
with Peter sitting as guard
under the Prince of Heaven.
Absolving our sins,
Grant us protection
Let the world resound with glory,
while Peter delivers the privileged
from mortal sin.

28

Carol: *Salve, sancta parens* (15th century)

John Stevens, ed., *Mediaeval Carols*, Musica Britannica, IV (London: Stainer & Bell, 1952), 71. Reprinted by permission.

stel - la ful - gens in__ sub - li - - mi si - dus e - ni - - - - - xa.

stel - la ful - gens in__ sub - li - - mi si - dus e - ni - - - - - xa.

Salve, sancta parens,	Hail, holy parent,
Enixa puerpera Regem.	from a woman in labor issued a King.
Salve, porta paradisi,	Hail, gate of paradise,
Felix atque fixa,	happy and firm,
Stella fulgens in sublimi	star shining on high
Sidus enixa.	from which a constellation sprang.

29

JOHN DUNSTABLE (CA. 1385–1453)
Motet: *Quam pulchra es*

Quam pul - cra es et quam de - co - ra, ca - ris - si - ma in

Quam pul - cra es et quam de - co - ra, ca - ris - si - ma in

Quam pul - cra es et quam de - co - ra, ca - ris - si - ma in

de - li - ci - is. Sta - tu - ra tu - a

de - li - ci - is. Sta - tu - ra tu - a as-

de - li - ci - is. Sta - tu - ra tu - a as-

Reprinted from Donald J. Grout, *History of Western Music*, revised edition, (New York, 1973), pp. 155–56.

as - si - mi - la - ta est pal - - - me,   et u - be - ra

si - mi - la - ta est pal - - - me,   et u - be - ra

si - mi - la - ta est pal - - - me,   et u - be - ra

tu - a bo - tris.   Ca - put tu - um   ut Car - me - lus,

tu - a bo - tris. Ca - put tu - um ut   Car - me - lus,

tu - a bo - tris.   Ca - put   tu - um ut Car - - me - lus, col -

col - lum tu - um si - cut   tur - - ris e - bur -

col - lum tu - um si - cut tur - - ris e - bur -

col - lum tu - um si - cut tur - - ris e - bur -

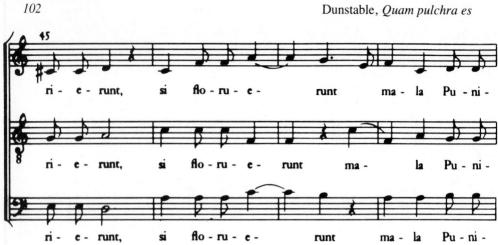

Quam pulchra es et quam decora,
    carissima in delicis.
Statuta tua assimilata est palme,
    et ubera tua botris.
Caput tuum ut Carmelus,
    collum tuum sicut turis eburnea.
Veni, dilecte mi,
    egrediamur in agrum,
et videamus si flores fructus parturierunt
    si floruerunt mala Punica.
Ibi dabo tibi ubera mea.
Alleluia.

How fair and how pleasant art thou,
    O love, for delights!
Thy stature is like to a palm tree, and
    thy breasts to clusters of grapes.
Thine head upon thee is like Carmel;
    thy neck is a tower of ivory.
Come, my beloved,
    let us go forth into the field . . .
And see whether the tender grapes appear and
    the pomegranates bud forth:
There will I give thee my loves.
Alleluia.

D. GROUT

30

GUILLAUME DUFAY (CA. 1400–74)
Hymn: *Conditor alme siderum*
(even verses, alternating with plainchant)

1 Con - di - tor al - me si - de - rum, Ae - ter - na lux cre - den - ti - um,
3 Ver - gen - te mun - di ves - pe - re U - ti spon - sus de tha - la - mo
5 Te de - pre - ca - mur a - gi - e Ven - tu - re iu - dex sae - cu - li

Chri - ste, red - em - ptor o - mni - um Ex - au - di pre - ces sup - pli - cum.
E - gres - sus ho - ne - stis - si - ma Vir - gi - nis ma - tris clau - su - la:
Con - ser - va nos in - tem - po - re Ho - stis a te - lo per - ti - di.

Faulx bourdon

2. Qui con - do - lens in te - ri - tu Mor -
4. Cu - jus for - ti po - ten - ti - ae Ge -
6. Laus, ho - nor, vir - tus, glo - ri - a De -

2. Qui con - do - lens in te - ri - tu Mor -
4. Cu - jus for - ti po - ten - ti - ae Ge -
6. Laus, ho - nor, vir - tus, glo - ri - a De -

Tenor

Qui condolens

2. tis per - i - re sae - cu - lum, Sol - va - sti mun - dum
4. nu cur - van - tur o - mni - a Coe - le - sti - a, ter -
6. o pa - tri et fi - li - o San - cto si - mul pa -

2. tis per - i - re sae - cu - lum, Sol - va - sti mun - dum
4. nu cur - van - tur o - mni - a Coe - le - sti - a, ter -
6. o pa - tri et fi - li - o San - cto si - mul pa -

Chant from *Antiphonale,* Appendix, pp. 11–12. Dufay, *Opera omnia*, ed. Heinrich Besseler, V (American Institute of Musicology, 1966), p. 39. Reprinted by permission of A. Carapetyan, Director and Hänssler-Verlag, West Germany. All rights reserved. International copyright secured.

2. lan - gui -	dum,	Do -	nans re -	is re - me - di - um.
4. re - stri -	a,	Nu -	tu fa -	ten - tur sub - di - ta.
6. ra - cli -	to	In	sae - cu -	lo - rum sae - cu - la.

2. lan - gui -	dum,	Do -	nans re -	is re - me - di - um.
4. re - stri -	a,	Nu -	tu fa -	ten - tur sub - di - ta.
6. ra - cli -	to	In	sae - cu -	lo - rum sae - cu - la.

A - men.

Conditor alme siderum,	Bountiful creator of the stars,
Aeterna lux credentium,	eternal light of believers,
Christe redemptor omnium	Christ, redeemer of all,
Exaudi preces supplicum.	hear the prayers of the supplicants.
Qui condolens interitu	You who suffer the ruin
Mortis perire saeculum,	of death, the perishing of the race,
Solvasti mundum languidum,	who saved the sick world,
Donans reis remedium:	bringing the healing balm.
Vergente mundi vespere	As the world turns toward evening,
Uti sponsus de thalamo,	the bridegroom from his chamber
Egressus honestissima	issues forth from the most chaste
Virginis matris clausula:	cloister of the Virgin mother.
Cujus forti potentiae	You, before whose mighty power
Genu curvantur omnia	all bend their knees,
Coelestia, terrestria,	celestial, terrestrial,
Nutu fatentur subdita.	confessing subjection to his command.
Te deprecamur agie	We entreat you, holy
Venture judex saeculi	judge of the days to come,
Conserva nos in tempore	save us in time
Hostis a telo perfidi.	from the weapons of the perfidious.
Laus, honor, virtus, gloria	Praise, honor, courage, glory,
Deo patri, et filio,	to God, the Father, and Son,
Sancto simul paraclito	and also to the Holy Protector,
in saeculorum saecula.	time everlasting, amen.

31

Guillaume Dufay

Motet: *Nuper rosarum flores* (1436)

This motet was composed for the consecration of the Cathedral of Santa Maria del Fiore in Florence by Pope Eugene IV on March 25, 1436. Chant from *LU*, p. 1250. Dufay, *Opera omnia,* ed. Heinrich Besseler, I (American Institute of Musicology, 1966), 70–75. Reprinted by permission of A. Carapetyan, Director and Hänssler-Verlag, West Germany. All rights reserved. International copyright secured.

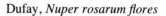

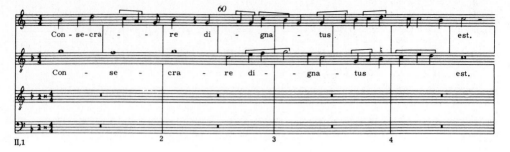

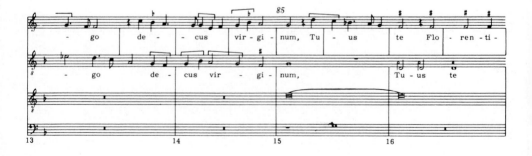

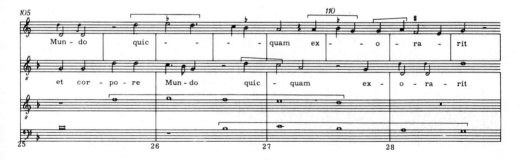

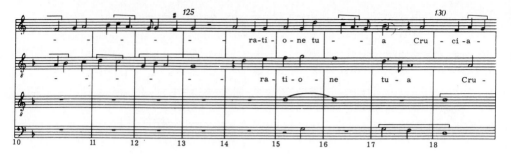

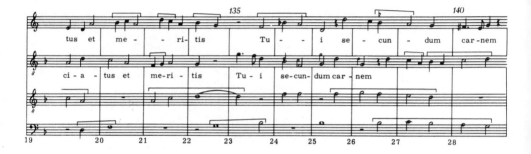

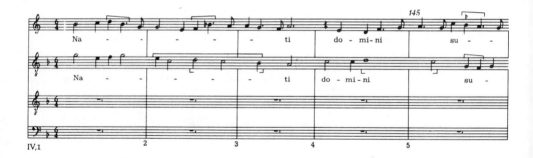

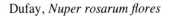

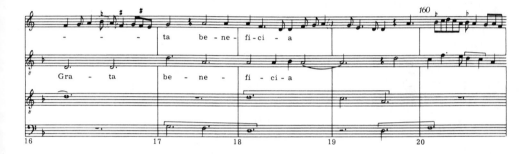

Nuper rosarum flores	Recently roses [came]
Ex dono pontificis	as a gift of the Pope,
Hieme licet horrida,	although in cruel winter,
Tibi, virgo coelica,	to you, heavenly Virgin.
Pie et sancte deditum	Dutifully and blessedly is dedicated
Grandis templum machinae	[to you] a temple of magnificent design.
Condecorarunt perpetim.	May they together be perpetual ornaments.
Hodie vicarius	Today the Vicar
Jesu Christi et Petri	of Jesus Christ and Peter's
Successor EUGENIUS	successor, Eugenius,
Hoc idem amplissimum	this same most spacious
Sacris templum manibus	sacred temple with his hands
Sanctisque liquoribus	and with holy waters
Consecrare dignatus est.	he is worthy to consecrate.
Igitur, alma parens,	Therefore, gracious mother
Nati tui et filia,	and daughter of your offspring,
Virgo decus virginum,	Virgin, ornament of virgins,
Tuus te FLORENTIAE	your, Florence's, people
Devotus orat populus,	devoutly pray
Ut qui mente et corpore	so that together with all mankind,
Mundo quicquam exoravit,	with mind and body, their entreaties may move you.
Oratione tua	Through your prayer,
Cruciatus et meritis	your anguish and merits,
Tui secundum carnem	may [the people] deserve to receive of the Lord,
Nati domini sui	born of you according to the flesh,
Grata beneficia	the benefits of grace
Veniamque reatum	and the remission of sins.
Accipere mereatur.	Amen.
Amen.	

Josquin des Prez (ca. 1440–1521)
Motet: *Tu solus, qui facis mirabilia*

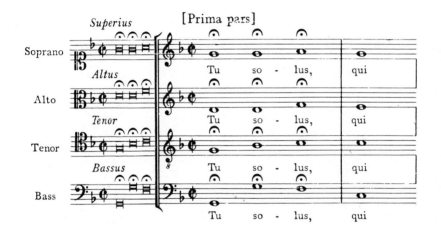

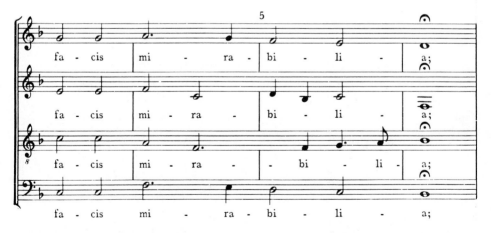

See No. 44 in this Anthology for Ockeghem's song, *D'ung aultre amer*, reworked in measures 56–72. *Motetti di passione* (Venice, 1503), ed. George Hunter in New York Pro Musica Series, no. 36 (New York/London: Associated Music Publishers, 1973, pp. 3–12. Reprinted by permission.

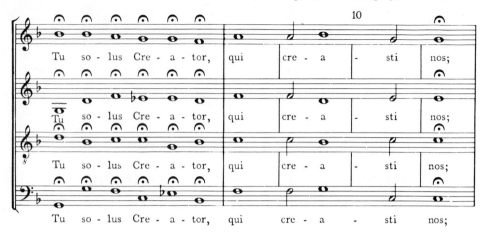

Tu so - lus Cre - a - tor, qui cre - a - sti nos;

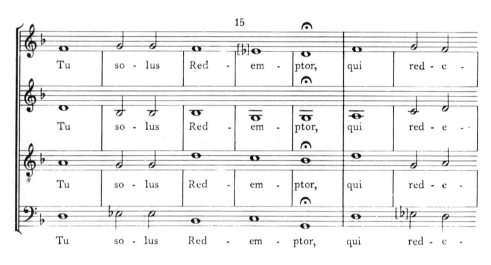

Tu so - lus Red - em - ptor, qui red - e -

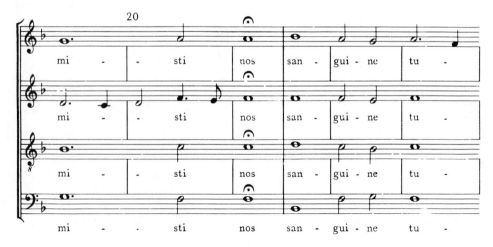

mi - sti nos san - gui - ne tu -

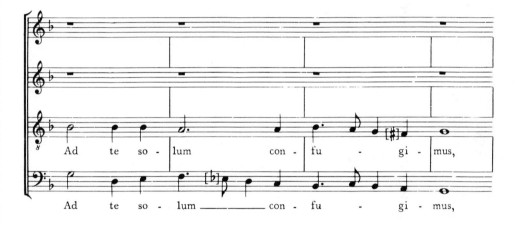

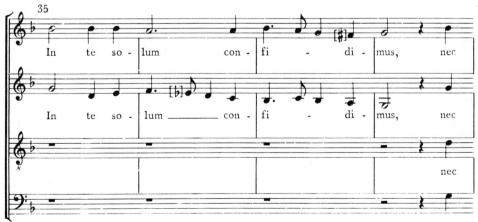

[Secunda pars]

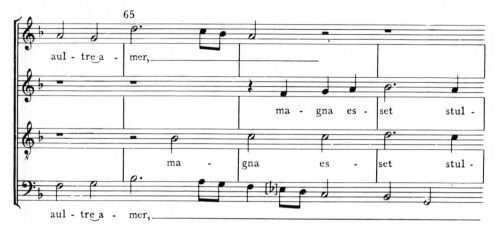

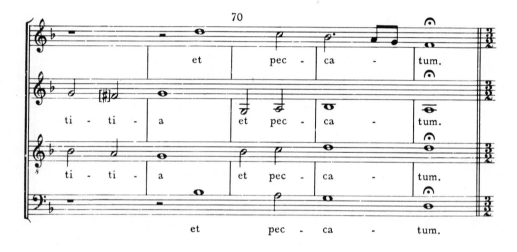

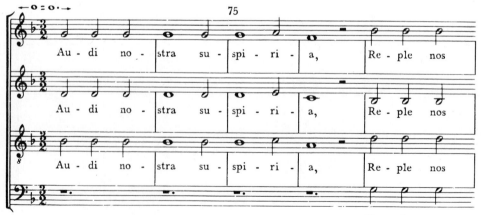

Tu solus, qui facis mirabilia;

Tu solus Creator, qui creastinos;

Tu solus Redemptor, qui redemisti nos

sanguine tuo pretiosissimo.

Ad te solum confugimus,

In te solum confidimus,

Nec alium adoramus, Jesu Christe.

Ad te preces effundimus,

Exaudi quod supplicamus,

Et concede quod petimus,

Rex benigne!

D'ung aultre amer, nobis esset fallacia;

D'ung aultre amer, magna esset stultitia et
peccatum.

Audi nostra suspiria,

Reple nos tua gratia, O Rex regum:

Ut ad tua servitia sistamus cum laetitia in
aeternum.

You only, who do wonders,

You, the only Creator, who created us,

You only are the Redeemer, who redeemed us
with

Your most precious blood.

In You alone we seek refuge,

in You alone we place our trust,

and no other do we adore, Jesus Christ.

To You we offer our prayers,

hear what we beg of You,

and grant what we request,

benign King.

To love another would be deceitful:

To love another would be great folly and sin.

Hear our sighs,

fill us with your grace, O king of kings,

that we may remain in your service with joy
forever.

Josquin des Prez

Motet: *Dominus regnavit*

Psalm 92 for Lauds

Tomus secundus psalmorum selectorum quatuor et quinque vocum (Nuremberg, 1539).
Josquin, *Werken*, ed. Albert J. Smijers, XVII (Amsterdam: G. Alsbach & Co., 1955), 33–40.
Used by permission of Vereniging voor Nederlandse Muziekgeschiedenis.

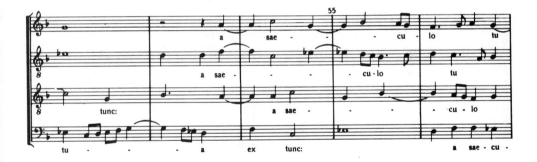

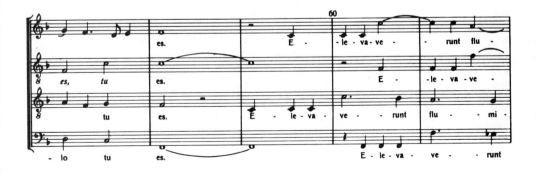

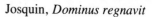

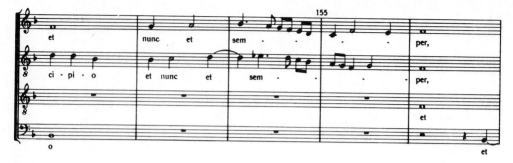

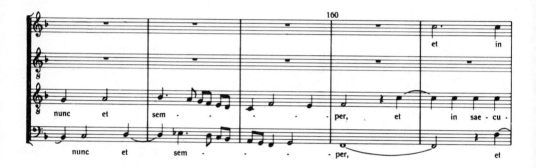

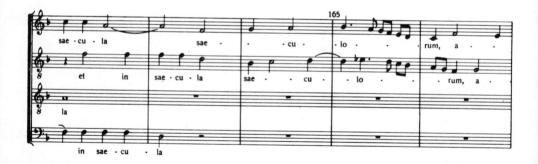

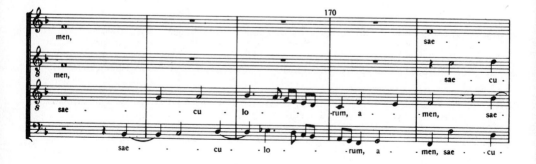

Dominus regnavit,
decorem indutus est:
indutus est Dominus fortitudinem,
et praecinxit se.
Etenim firmavit orbem terrae,
qui non commovebitur.
Parata sedes tua ex tunc:
a saeculo tu es.
Elevaverunt flumina, Domine:
elevaverunt flumina vocem suam.
Elevaverunt flumina fluctus suos,
a vocibus aquarum multarum.

Mirabiles elationes maris:
mirabilis in altis Dominus.
Testimonia tua credibilia facta sunt nimis:
domum tuam decet sanctitudo, Domine,
in longitudine dierum.
Gloria Patri et Filio,
et Spiritui Sancto.
Sicut erat in principio, et nunc, et semper,
et in saecula saeculorum, amen.

The Lord reigneth,
He is clothed with majesty;
the Lord is clothed with strength,
wherewith He hath girded himself:
the world also is established,
so that it will not be moved.
Thy throne is established of old:
Thou art from everlasting.
The floods have lifted up, O Lord,
the floods have lifted up their voice;
the floods lift up their waves,
from the sound of many waters.

As mighty as the waves of the sea
the Lord on high is mightier.
Thy testimonies are very sure:
holiness becometh thine house, O Lord
forever.
Glory be to the Father and the Son,
and the Holy Spirit.
As it was in the beginning so it ever shall be,
world without end, amen.

Adapted from the King James Version
of Psalm 93

Jean Mouton (1459–1522)
Motet: *Noe, noe*

See p. 198 for Arcadelt's Mass built upon this motet. Pierre Attaingnant, ed., Liber secundus: 24 musicales quatuor vocum Motets (Paris, 1534). Arcadelt, Opera omnia. ed. Albert Seay, I (American Institute of Musicology, 1965), 82–86.

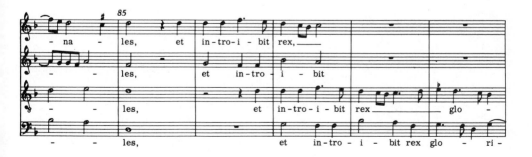

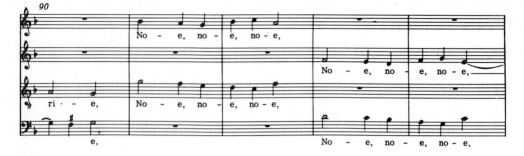

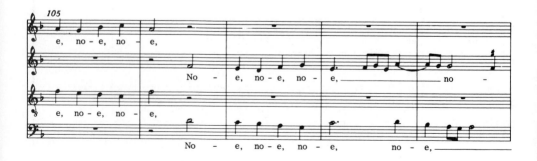

Noe, noe, psallite noe,
Jherusalem, gaude et letare,
quia hodie natus est Salvator mundi.
Jacet in praesepio, fulget in celo.
Attolite portas, principes, vestras,
et elevamini, porte eternales,
et introibit rex glorie.
Quis est iste rex glorie?
Dominus virtutum ipse est rex glorie.

Noel, noel, sing and play noel.
Jerusalem, rejoice and be glad,
for today was born the Savior of the world.
He lies in the manger, he shines in the sky.
Lift up your gates, Princes,
and be lifted up, eternal gates,
and the King of Glory will enter.
Who is this King of Glory?
The Lord of powers, he is himself the King of
    Glory.

ADRIAN WILLAERT (CA. 1490–1562)
Motet: *O crux, splendidior cunctis astris*
Antiphon at First Vespers, The Finding of the Holy Cross

At Magn.
Ant. 1. D

O Crux, * splendí-di- or cúnctis ástris, múndo cé-lebris, homí-ni-bus multum amá-bi- lis, sán- cti- or u-nivér-sis : quae só-la fu- ísti dígna portá- re ta-léntum múndi : dúlce lígnum, dúlces clávos, dúlci- a férens póndera : sál- va praeséntem ca-térvam, in tú- is hódi- e láudibus congre-gá-tam. *T. P.* Alle- lú- ia, alle- lú- ia. E u o u a e.

Antiphon: *LU*, 1453. Willaert, *Musica quinque vocum . . . vulgo Motecta . . . Liber primus* (Venice, 1539). *Opera omnia,* ed. Hermann Zenck, III (American Institute of Musicology, 1950), 66–72. Reprinted by permission of A. Carapetyan, Director and Hänssler-Verlag, West Germany. All rights reserved. International copyright secured.

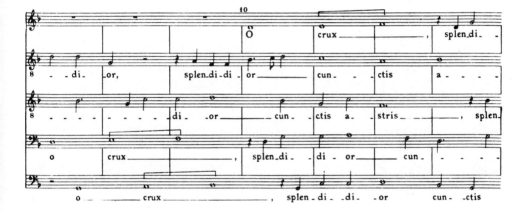

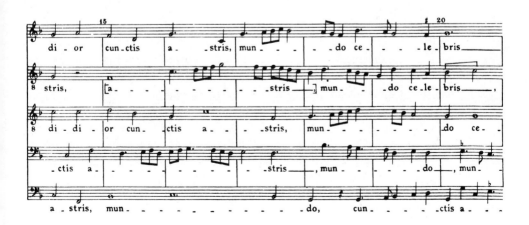

SECUNDA PARS

O crux,
splendidior cunctis astris,
mundo celebris,
hominibus multum amabilis,
sanctior universis:
quae sola fuisti digna
portare talentum mundi.
Dulce lignum,
dulces clavos,
dulcia ferens pondera:
salve praesenten capervam
in tuis hodie laudibus congregatam,
Alleluia.

O cross,
shining more brightly than all stars,
renowned throughout the world,
much beloved by mankind,
holier than all creation:
you alone were worthy
to bear the treasure of the world.
Sweet wood,
sweet nails,
bearing your sweet burden:
save this group,
gathered before you today to praise you.
Alleluia.

CHRISTÓBAL DE MORALES (CA. 1500–53)
Motet: *Emendemus in melius*

Cristóbal de Morales, *Opera omnia,* ed. Higinio Anglés, 8:73–78. Monumentos de la música española, 34 (Rome: Escuela española de historia y arqueologa en Roma. Instituto español de musicologa, Consejo superior de investigacione cientficas, Delegación de Roma, 1971). Used by permission.

Emendemus in melius, quae
ignoranter peccavimus: ne subito
praeocupati die mortis,
quaeramus spatium paenitentiae, et
invenire non possimus. Attende
Domine, et miserere: quia
peccavimus tibi.

Memento homo quia pulvis est, et in
pulverem reverteris.

Let us make amends for unknowingly
sinning, lest suddenly,
worried on the day of death,
we seek a place of repentance and
cannot find one. Listen to us,
Lord, and have pity, because we
have sinned against you.

Remember man, "you are dust,
and to dust you shall return."
(Quotation from Gen. 3:19)

ORLANDO DI LASSO (1532–94)
Motet: *Cum essem parvulus* (1579)

Motetta sex vocum (Munich, 1582). The motet is inscribed "August 1579" in Munich, Staatsbibliothek, Ms. 11 The text is from Epistle of St. Paul, I Corinthians 13: 11–13.

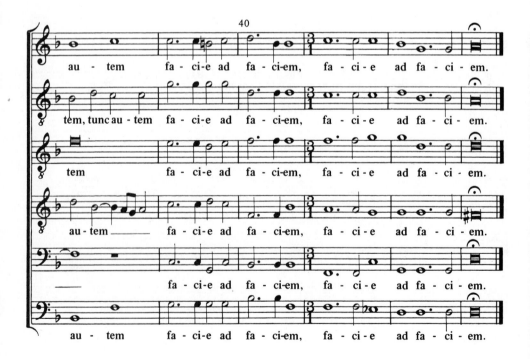

Secunda pars

Cum essem parvulus,
loquebar ut parvulus,
sapiebam ut parvulus,
cogitabam ut parvulus;
quando autem factus sum vir,
evacuavi quae erant parvuli.
Videmus nunc per speculum
in aenigmate; tunc autem
facie ad faciem.

Nunc cognosco ex parte,
tunc autem cognoscam
sicut et cognitus sum.
Fides, Spes, Charitas, tria haec:
major autem horum est Charitas.

When I was a child,
I spoke as a child,
I understood as a child,
I thought as a child;
but when I became a man,
I put away childish things.
Now we see through a mirror
in riddles; but then
face to face.

Now I understand in part;
then I shall understand [fully]
just as I shall be understood.
Faith, hope, love, these three:
but the greatest of these is love.

WILLIAM BYRD (1543–1623)
Motet: *Tu es petrus*

Gradualia seu cantionum sacrarum (London, 1607). The text is from Matthew 16: 18. With the permission of Oxford University Press.

- si - am me - am, Ec - cle - si-am me - - -
am, Ec-cle - si-am me - - am, ae -
et su-per hanc pe - tram ae - di - fi-ca-bo Ec - cle-si-
ae - di-fi-ca-bo Ec - cle - si-am me - am,
di-fi-ca-bo Ec-cle - si - am me - am, Ec - cle - si-am
tram,
et su - per hanc
10
am, ae - di - fi-ca-bo Ec-cle - si-am me - - -
di - fi-ca-bo Ec - cle - si - am me - - am,
am me - am, Ec - cle - si - am me - am, et su-per hanc
ae - di - fi-ca-bo Ec - cle - si-am, ae - di - fi-ca-bo Ec-cle - si-am me -
me - am, ae - di - fi-ca-bo Ec-cle - si-am me -
pe - - - - - tram,

Tu es Petrus, et super hanc petram,
aedificabo Ecclesiam meam.
Alleluia.

You are Peter, and on this rock
will build my church.
Alleluia.

39

GUILLAUME DUFAY

Se la face ay pale

a) Ballade: *Se la face ay pale*, arrangement for three voices by Dufay

Se la face ay pale,	If my face is pale,
La cause est amer,	the cause is love,
Et tant m'est amer	and it is so bitter for me
Amer, qu'en la mer	to love, that in the sea
Me voudroye voir;	I would throw myself.
Or, scet bien de voir	Then would she see—
La belle a qui suis	the fair lady to whom I belong—
Que nul bien avoir	that no joy can I have
Sans elle ne puis.	without her.

Guillaume Dufay, *Opera omnia*, ed. Heinrich Besseler, Corpus mensurabilis musicae 1 (American Institute of Musicology, 1951–66) 6:36 (Ballade); 3:5–13 (Mass). Reprinted by permission of A. Carapetyan, Director and Hänssler-Verlag, West German All rights reserved. International copyright secured.

b) *Missa Se la face ay pale: Gloria*

40

Johannes Ockeghem (ca. 1420–97)
Missa Caput: Agnus Dei

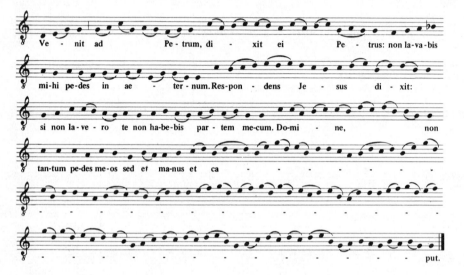

Ve - nit ad Pe - trum, di - xit ei Pe - trus: non la-va-bis

mi-hi pe-des in ae - ter-num. Res-pon - dens Je - sus di - xit:

si non la-ve - ro te non ha-be-bis par - tem me-cum. Do-mi - ne, non

tan-tum pe-des me-os sed et ma-nus et ca - - - - -

- - - - - - - - put.

Antiphon, *Venit ad Petrum*, for Maundy Thursday, according to Sarum rite from *ibid.*, p. viii, the source for which is British Library, MS Harley 2942, fols. 48r–48v.

Alejandro Enrique Planchart, ed., *Missae Caput*, Collegium Musicum, No. 5 (New Haven: Yale University, 1964), pp. 90–97.

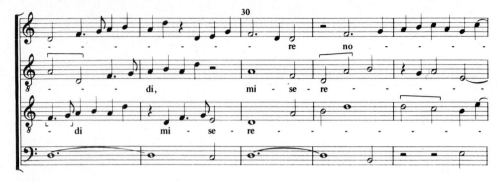

Jacob Obrecht (ca. 1450–1505)
Missa Caput: Agnus Dei

Alejandro Enrique Planchart, ed., *Missae Caput,* (see note No. 40), pp. 176–82.

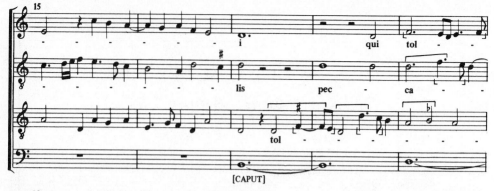

[CAPUT]

JOHN TAVERNER (CA. 1490–1545)
Missa Gloria tibi trinitas: Benedictus

Note values quartered. See p. 288 for an "In nomine" based on the same cantus firmus. Antiphon for Second Vespers, Trinity Sunday: *Antiphonale Sarisburense*, ed. W. H. Frere (London: Plainsong and Mediaeval Music Society, 1901–25), p. 286. Mass: *John Taverner: 1. Six-Part Masses*, ed. Hugh Benham (London: Stainer and Bell, 1978), pp. 55–60. Reprinted by permission of Stainer and Bell, Ltd. and the Musica Britannica Trust, London, England.

For a translation of the text see p. 17.

Jacob Arcadelt (ca. 1505–68)
Missa Noe noe: Kyrie and Gloria

Values halved. See p. 130, Mouton's motet, *Noe, noe,* upon which this Mass is based. *Missae tres Jacobo Arcadelt* (Paris, 1557). Albert Seay, ed., Arcadelt, *Opera omnia,* I (American Institute of Musicology, 1965), 1–8. Reprinted by permission of A. Carapetyan, Director, and Hänssler-Verlag, West Germany. All rights reserved. International copyright secured.

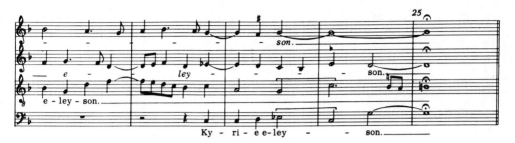

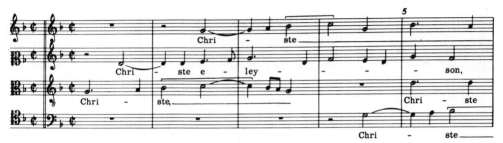

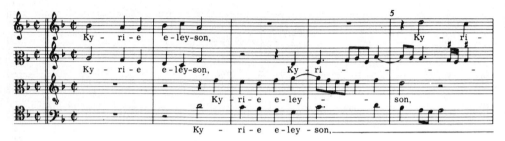

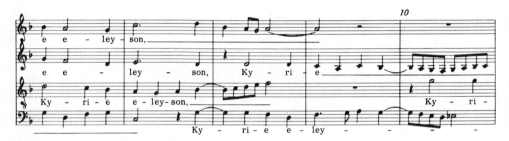

Et in terra pax hominibus bonae voluntatis.	And on earth peace to men of good will.
Laudamus te. Benedicimus te. Adoramus te. Glorificamus te.	We praise thee, we bless thee, we adore thee, we glorify thee.
Gratias agimus tibi propter magnam gloriam tuam.	We give thee thanks for thy great glory.
Domine Deus, Rex caelestis,	O Lord God, King of heaven,
Deus Pater omnipotens.	God the Father almighty.
Domine Fili unigenite Jesu Christe.	O Lord, the only begotten Son, Jesus Christ.
Domine Deus, Agnus Dei, Filius Patris.	O Lord God, Lamb of God, Son of the Father.
Qui tollis peccata mundi, miserere nobis.	Thou who takest away the sins of the world, have mercy on us.
Qui tollis peccata mundi, suscipe deprecationem nostram.	Thou who takest away the sins of the world, receive our prayer.
Qui sedes ad dexteram Patris,	Thou who sittest at the right hand of the Father,
miserere nobis.	have mercy on us.
Quoniam tu solus sanctus.	For thou only art holy,
Tu solus Dominus.	Thou only art Lord.
Tu solus Altissimus, Jesu Christe.	Thou only art most high, O Jesus Christ,
Cum Sancto Spiritu,	With the Holy Ghost,
In Gloria Dei Patris. Amen.	In the glory of God the Father. Amen.

For a translation of the *Kyrie*, see p. 14.

Giovanni da Palestrina (ca. 1525–94)
Pope Marcellus Mass: Credo

Missarum Liber secundus (Rome, 1567). *Opere complete di Giovanni Pierluigi da Palestrina,* ed. Raffaele Casimiri (Rome: Edizione Fratelli-Scalera), IV (1939), 177–87. Reprinted by permission of the Instituto Italiano per la Storia Della Musica.

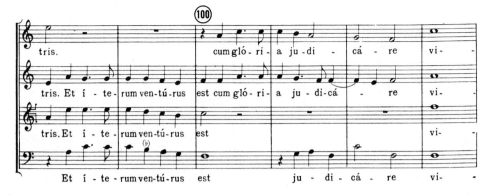

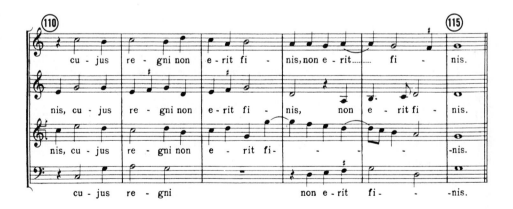

For a translation of the text, see p. 16.

45

GUILLAUME DUFAY

Ballade: *Resvellies vous et faites chiere lye*

(1423)

Opera omnia, ed. Heinrich Besseler, VI (American Institute of Musicology, 1964), pp. 25–26. Reprinted by permission of A. Carapetyan, Director and Hänssler-Verlag, West Germany. All rights reserved. International copyright secured.

Resvellies vous et faites chiere lye
Tout amoureux qui gentilesse ames
Esbates vous, fuyes merancolye,
De bien servir point ne soyes hodés
Car au jour d'ui sera li espousés,
Par grant honneur et noble seignourie;
Ce vous convient ung chascum faire feste,
Pour bien grignier la belle compagnye;
Charle gentil, c'on dit de Maleteste.

Il a dame belle et bonne choysie,
Dont il sera grandement honnourés;
Car elle vient de tres noble lignie
Et de barons qui sont mult renommés.
Son propre nom est Victoire clamés;
De la colonne vient sa progenie.
C'est bien rayson qu'a vascule requeste
De cette dame mainne bonne vie.
Charle gentil, c'on dit de Maleteste.

Awake and be merry,
lovers all who love gentleness;
frolic and flee melancholy.
Tire not of serving yourself well,
for today will be the nuptials,
with great honor and noble lordship,
and it behooves you, everyone, to celebrate
and join the happy company.
Noble *Charles,* who is named *Malatesta.*

He has chosen a lady, fair and good,
by whom he will be greatly honored,
for she comes from a very noble lineage
of barons who are much renowned.
Her name is *Victoria,*
and she descends from the *Collonas.*
It is right, therefore, that his appeal be heard
to live honestly with this lady.
Noble *Charles,* who is named *Malatesta.*

46

Guillaume Dufay

Rondeau: *Adieu ces bons vins de Lannoys*
(1426)

Opera omnia, ed. Heinrich Besseler, VI (American Institute of Musicology, 1964), 50. Reprinted by permission of A. Carapetyan, Director and Hänssler-Verlag, West Germany. All rights reserved. Internationai copyright secured.

Adieu ces bons vins de Lannoys,
Adieu dames, adieu borgois,
Adieu celle que tant amoye,
Adieu toute playsante joye
Adieu tous compaignons galois.

Je m'en vois tout arquant des nois,
Car je ne truis feves ne pois,
Dont bien souvent [. . .]-ier mennoye.

Adieu ces bons vins de Lannoys,
Adieu dames, adieu borgois,
Adieu celle que tant amoye.

De moy seres, par plusieurs fois
Regretés par dedans les bois,
Ou il n'y a sentier ne voye;
Puis ne scaray que faire doye,
Se je ne crie a haute vois.
Adieu ces bons vins de Lannoys, etc.

Farewell, these good wines of Lannoy.
Farewell, ladies, farewell townsfolk.
Farewell to her whom I loved so well.
Farewell all pleasurable joy.
Farewell all my Welsh companions.

I find myself searching for nuts,
because I cannot find beans or peas,
which very often makes me annoyed.

Farewell, these good wines of Lannoy.
Farewell ladies, farewell townsfolk.
Farewell to her whom I loved so well.

By me you will be often
missed, deep in the woods
where there is no path or way;
then I shall not know what I should do
unless I shout in a loud voice.
Farewell, these good wines of Lannoy.

47

WILLIAM CORNYSH (CA. 1465–1523)
Partsong: *My love she mourneth* (1426)

Music at the Court of Henry VIII, transcribed and edited by John Stevens, in *Musica Britannica* 18:23 (London: publ. for the Royal Musical Association by Stainer & Bell Ltd., 1962). Reproduced by permission of Stainer & Bell, Ltd. and the Musica Britannica Trust, London, England.

48

Johannes Ockeghem

Chanson: *D' ung aultre amer mon cueur s'abesseroit*

See Josquin's motet, *Tu solus*, p. 113, which is partly based on this song. Albert Smijers, ed., *Von Ockeghem tot Sweelinck* (Amsterdam: G. Alsbach & Co., 1952), II, 12. Used by permission of Vereniging voor Nederlandse Muziekgeschiedenis.

D'ung aultre amer mon cueur s'abesseroit,
Il ne fault pas penser que je l'estrange,

Ne que pour rien de ce propos me change.

Car mon honneur en appetisseroit.

Je l'aime tant que jamais ne seroit
Possible a moy d'en consentir l'echange.
D'ung aultre amer . . . (etc.)

La mort, par Dieu, avant me defferoit,
Qu'en mon vivant j'acointasse ung estrange.

Ne cuide nul qu'a cela je me renge,
Ma loyaulté trop fort se mesferoit.
D'ung aultre amer . . . (etc.)

To love another my heart would be debased.
It should not be thought that I estrange myself
    from him,
or that anything would bend me from this re-
    solve,
because my honor would be in jeopardy.

I love him so much that never would it be
possible for me to consent to an exchange.
To love another . . . (etc.)

Death, by God, would sooner unlock me
than that in my lifetime I should know a
    stranger.
Think not that I would adapt myself to this.
My fidelity would be too much damaged.
To love another . . . (etc.)

49

JOSQUIN DES PREZ
Mille regretz

a) Vocal chanson in four parts

First published in a lute arrangement by Hans Newsidler, *Ein New geordnet Künstlich Lautenbuch* (Nuremberg, 1536). Reprinted by permission of the publishers from *The Chanson and Madrigal*, edited by James Haar. Cambridge, Mass.: Harvard University Press, © 1968 by the President and Fellows of Harvard College.

Mille regretz de vous habandonner
Et d'eslonger vostre fache amoureuse,
Jay si grand dueil et paine douloureuse,

Quon me verra brief mes jours definer.

A thousand regrets at deserting you
and leaving behind your loving face,
I feel so much sadness and such painful distress,

that it seems to me my days will soon dwindle away.

b) Arrangement for vihuela by Luis de Narváez (after ca. 1500–after ca. 1555)

Narváez, *Los seys libros del Delphin de música de cifras para vihuela* (Valladolid, 1538). In this source the song is named "La cancion del Emperador," and may have been among "aucunes chanssons nouvelles" delivered by Josquin to Charles V in September 1520. See *MGG*, vii, 197. Edited by Geneviève Thibault in "Instrumental Transcriptions of Josquin's French Chansons," in *Josquin des Prez*, ed. Edward E. Lowinsky (London: Oxford University Press, 1976), pp. 464–66.

50

Lied: *Nu bitten wir heil'gen Geist*

Nu bit - ten wir den heil'-gen geist umb

den rech - ten glau - ben al - ler - meist,

daß er uns be - hü - te an un-serm en - de,

so wir heim - farn aus die - sem e - len - de. Ky - ri - e

Glogauer Liederbuch, Berlin, Deutsche Staatsbibliothek, MS 40098 Z. 98. Reprinted by permission of Bärenreiter-Verlag, Kassel, Basel, Tours, London, from *Das Erbe deutscher Musik,* IV, edited by H. Ringmann and J. Klapper. (Kassel, etc., 1954), 5.

Nu bitten wir den heil'gen Geist
umb den rechten Glauben allermeist,
dass er uns behüte an unserm Ende,
so wir heimfarn aus diesem Elende.
Kyrie eleison.

Now we pray to the Holy Ghost
for the true faith most of all,
that He may watch over us at our end,
when we shall go homeward from this misery.
Kyrie eleison.

Canto carnascialesco: *Orsu, car' Signori*

51

Johannes Wolf, ed., *Sing- und Spielmusik aus älterer Zeit* (Leipzig: Verlag von Quelle & Meyer, 1931), pp. 49–51.

Orsù, orsu, car' Signori,
Chi soe bolle vol spedire,
Venga ad nui che siam scripturi.
Sù, Signori se volete
Vostre bolle far spacciare.
Et se ad nui le manderete,
Novelle farem stentare.
Ma volemo pacto fare,
Despacciare soct'a sopra.
Octo el giorno et far bona opra.
Quanto faccia altri scripturi.

Step up, dear sirs,
if you wish your bulls quickly certified.
Come to us, for we are scribes.
Come up, sirs, if you wish to
have your bulls made ready.
And if you consign them to us,
we shall not make you wait.
We want to come to terms,
and do them right, above and below.
Eight a day, and good work, too,
as good as other scribes.

Ogni cosa in punto et bene	Every detail will be just right
Et in ordine tenemo.	and in good order.
Per servire chi prima vene	To serve whomever first arrives
Nostra penna in man piglemo.	we take pen in hand.
Nel calamaro la mectemo	We dip it in the ink-well
Et cacciamo for' l'ingiostro.	and we press the ink out.
Se provate el servire nostro,	If you try our service,
Non vorrete altri scripturi.	you'll not want other scribes.
Orsu, orsu, car' Signori,	Step up, dear sirs,
Chi soe bolle vol spedire	if you wish your bulls quickly certified.
Venga ad nui che siam scripturi.	Come to us, for we are scribes.

52

Heinrich Isaac (ca. 1450–1517)
Lied: *Innsbruck, ich muss dich lassen*

a) *Gross Leid muss ich jetzt tragen*

52a, textless in the sources, has been reconstructed from two manuscripts; the second stanza of the Lied has been set to the parts; 52b from G. Forster, *Ein ausszug guter alter und newer teutscher Liedlein* (Nuremberg, 1539).
Noah Greenberg and Paul Maynard, *An Anthology of Early Renaissance Music* (New York, 1975), pp. 181–84.

b) *Innsbruck, ich muss dich lassen*

be - kom - men, wo ich im E - lend

be-kom - men, wo ich im E - lend

be-kom - men, wo ich im E - lend

be - kom - men, wo ich im E - lend, im E - lend

bin, wo ich im E - lend bin.

bin, wo ich im E - lend bin.

bin, wo ich im E - lend bin.

bin, wo ich im E - lend bin.

Innsbruck, ich muss dich lassen,	Innsbruck, I must leave you
ich fahr dahin mein Strassen,	I am going on my way
in fremde Land dahin.	into a foreign land.
Mein Freud is mir genommen,	My joy is taken from me,
die ich nit weiss bekommen,	I know not how to regain it,
wo ich im Elend bin.	while in such misery.
Gross Leid muss ich jetzt tragen,	I must now endure great pain
das ich allein tu klagen	which I confide only
dem liebsten Buhlen mein.	to my dearest love.
Ach Lieb, nun lass mich Armen	O beloved, find pity
im Herzen dein erbarmen,	in your heart for me,
dass ich muss dannen sein.	that I must part from you.
Mein Trost ob allen Weiben,	My comfort above all other women,
dein tu ich ewig bleiben,	I shall always be yours,
stet treu, der Ehren fromm.	forever faithful in honor true.
Nun muss dich Gott bewahren,	May the good Lord protect you
in aller Tugend sparen,	and keep you in your virtue
bis dass ich wiederkomm.	for me, till I return.

N. GREENBERG and P. MAYNARD

53

CLAUDIN DE SERMISY (CA. 1490–1562)

Chanson: *Tant que vivray en aage florissant*

Tant que vivray en aage florissant,	As long as I am able bodied,
Je serviray d'amours le roy puissant	I shall serve the potent king of love
En fais enditz en chansons et accordz.	through deeds, words, songs, and harmonies.
Par plusieurs fois m'a tenu languissant,	Many times he made me languish,

Mais apres deul m'a faict rejoyssant	but after mourning, he let me rejoice,
Car j'ay l'amour de la belle au gent corps.	because I have the love of the fair lady with the lovely body.
Son alliance	Her alliance
C'est ma fiance,	is my betrothal.
Son cueur est mien,	Her heart is mine,
Le mien est sien.	mine is hers.
Fy de tristesse,	Shun sorrow.
Vive lyesse,	Live in merriment,
Puisqu'en amour a tant de bien.	because there is so much good in love.
Quand je la veulx servir et honorer,	When I want to serve and honor her,
Quand par escriptz veulx son nom decorer,	when I want to adorn her name with words,
Quand je la veoy et visite souvent,	when I see and visit her often,
Ses envieux n'en font que murmurer;	those jealous of her do nothing but whisper;
Mais nostre amour n'en scauroit moins durer;	but our love would not last any less,
Autant ou plus en emporte le vent,	however far the wind carries the rumors.
Maulgré envie,	Despite jealousy,
Toute ma vie,	all my life,
Je l'aymeray	I will love her
Et chanteray;	and sing of her;
C'est la premiere,	She is the first,
C'est la derniere	she is the last
Que j'ay servie	that I have served
Et serviray.	and will serve.

CLÉMENT MAROT (CA. 1496–ca. 1544)

54

CLAUDE LE JEUNE
Chanson: *Revecy venir du printans*

RECHANT à 5

Le Printemps (Paris: Ballard, 1603). Ed. Henry Expert in *Les maîtres musiciens de la Renaissance française* 12 (Paris: Alphonse Leduc, 1900):11–27.

L'a _ mou _ reuz' et bel _ le sai _ zon.

L'a _ mou _ reuz' et bel _ le sai _ zon.

L'a _ mou _ reuz' et bel _ le sai _ zon.

L'a _ mou _ reuz' et bel _ le sai _ zon.

L'a _ mou _ reuz' et bel _ le sai _ zon.

[1] CHANT à 2

Dessus

Haute-Contre

Le cou _ rant des eaus re _ cher _ chant

Le cou _ rant des eaus re _ cher _ chant

Le ca _ nal dé té s'é _ clair _ cît:

Le ca _ nal dé té s'é _ clair _ cît:

Et la mer cal _ me de ces flots

Et la mer cal _ me de ces flots

A _ mo _ lit le tris _ te cour _ rous:
A _ mo _ li le tris _ te cour _ rous:

Le Ca _ nard s'e _ gay _ e plon _ jant,
Le Ca _ nard s'e _ gay _ e plon _ jant,

Et se la _ ve coint de _ dans l'eau:
Et se la _ ve coint de _ dans l'eau:

Et la grû' qui four _ che son vol
Et la grû' qui four _ che son vol

Re _ tra _ ver _ se l'air et s'en va.
Re _ tra _ ver _ se l'air et s'en va.

RECHANT à 5

[2] CHANT à 3

Dessus

Le So _ leil é _ clai _ re lui _ zant

Cinquiesme

Le So _ leil é _ clai _ re lui _ zant

Taille

Le 'So _ leil é _ clai _ re lui _ zant

D'u _ ne plus sé _ rei _ ne clair _ té:

D'u _ ne plus sé _ rei _ ne clair _ té:

D'u _ ne plus sé _ rei _ ne clair _ té:

Du nu _ a _ ge l'om _ bre s'en _ fuit,

Du nu _ a _ ge l'om _ bre s'en _ fuit,

Du nu _ a _ ge l'om _ bre s'en _ fuit,

RECHANT à 5

[3] CHANT à 4

CE RESTE est à 5

Ri _ on aus _ si nous: et cher _ chon

Ri _ on aus _ si nous: et cher _ chon

Ri _ on aus _ si nous: et cher _ chon

Ri _ on aus _ si nous: et cher _ chon

Ri _ on aus _ si nous: et cher _ chon

Les é _ bas et ieus du Prin _ tans:

Les é _ bas et ieus du Prin _ tans:

Les é _ bas et ieus du Prin _ tans:

Les é _ bas et ieus du Prin _ tans:

Les é _ bas et ieus du Prin _ tans:

(*) Dans l'original, par erreur:

Les é _ bas et

(*) Dans l'orig.

Revecy venir du Printans
L'amoureuz' et belle saizon.

Le courant des eaus recherchant
Le canal d'été s'éclaircît:
Et la mer calme de ces flots
Amolit le triste courrous:
Le Canard s'egaye plonjant,
Et se lave coint dedans l'eau;
Et la grû' qui fourche son vol
Retraverse l'air et s'en va.

Here again comes the Spring,
the amorous and fair season.

The currents of water that seek
the canal in summer become clearer;
and the calm sea the waves'
sad anger soothes.
The duck, elated, dives
and washes itself quietly in the water.
And the crane that branches off in flight
recrosses the air and flies away.

Revecy venir du Printans
L'amoureuz' et belle saizon.

Le Soleil éclaire luizant
D'une plus séreine clairté:
Du nuage l'ombre s'enfuit,
Qui se ioû' et court et noircît.
Et foretz et champs et coutaus
Le labeur humain reverdît,
Et la prê' découvre ses fleurs.

Revecy venir du Printans·
L'amoureuz' et belle saizon.

De Venus le filz Cupidon
L'univers semant de ses trais,
De sa flamme va réchaufér,
Animaus, qui volet en l'air,
Animaus, qui rampet au chams,
Animaus, qui naget auz eaus.
Ce qui mesmement ne sent pas,
Amoureux se fond de plaizir.

Revecy venir du Printans
L'amoureuz' et belle saizon.

Rion aussi nous: et cherchon
Les ébas et ieus du Printans:
Toute chose rit de plaizir:
Sélebron la gaye saizon,

Revecy venir du Printans
L'amoureuz' et belle saizon.

Revecy venir . . . .

Here again comes the Spring,
the amorous and fair season.

The sun shines brightly
with a calmer light.
The shadow of the cloud vanishes
from him who sports and runs and darkens.
Forests and fields and slopes
human labor makes green again,
and the prairie unveils its flowers.

Here again comes the Spring,
the amorous and fair season.

Cupid, the son of Venus
seeding the universe with his arrows,
with his flame he will rekindle
animals that fly in the air,
animals that crawl in the fields,
animals that swim in the seas.
Even those that feel not
in love they melt in pleasure.

Here again comes the Spring,
the amorous and fair season.

Let us, too, laugh, and let us seek
the sports and games of Spring:
everything smiles with pleasure
let us celebrate the merry season.

Here again comes the Spring,
the amorous and fair season.

Here again comes . . . .

55

MARCO CARA (SECOND HALF 15TH CENTURY–AFTER 1525)

Frottola: *Io non compro più speranza*

Io non com - pro più spe - ran - za Ché gli è fal - sa mercan - ci - a.

A dar sol at - ten - do vi - a Quella po - ca che m'a - van - za.

Io non com - pro più spe - ran - za Ché gli è fal - sa mer - can -

Note values halved. Notes in the lute part with dots under them are played with an upward stroke. Bars through the lute staves are original. Those between the voice part and lute accompaniment are added by the present editor to show the true metrical organization. Franciscus Bossinensis, ed., *Tenori e contrabassi intabulati col sopran in canto figurato per cantar e sonar col lauto, libro primo* (Venice, 1509). Benvenuto Disertori, ed., *Le Frottole per canto e liuto intabulate da Franciscus Bossinensis* (Milan: Ricordi, 1964), pp. 390–91. Reprinted by permission.

che gli è fal_sa mer_can_ci _

a.

letterale   letterale

Io non compro più speranza	I'll buy no more hope,
Ché gli è falsa mercancia	which is fake goods;
A dar sol attendo via	I can't wait to give away
Quella poca che m'avanza.	the little that I have left.
Io non compro più speranza	I'll buy no more hope,
Ché gli è falsa mercancia.	which is fake goods.
Cara un tempo la comprai,	Once I bought it dear;
Hor la vendo a bon mercato	now I sell it cheap;
E consiglio ben che mai	and I would advise that never
Non ne compri un sventurato	should the wretched buy it;
Ma più presto nel suo stato	rather let them in their condition
Se ne resti con costanza.	remain in constancy.
Io non . . .	I'll buy . . .
El sperare è come el sogno	To hope is like a dream
Che per più riesce in nulla,	that mostly results in nothing,
El sperar è proprio il bisogno	and hoping is the craving need
De chi al vento si trastulla,	of him who plays with the wind.
El sperare sovente anulla	Hoping often annihilates
Chi continua la sua danza.	the one who continues its dance.
Io non . . .	I'll buy . . .

56

Jacob Arcadelt
Madrigal: *Ahime, dov'è 'l bel viso*

Values halved. *Il primo libro di Madrigali d'Archadelt a quatro con nuova gionta impressi* (Venice, 1539; first edition lost but probably from 1538). Albert Seay, ed., Arcadelt, *Opera omnia*, II (American Institute of Musicology, 1970), 1–3. Reprinted by permission of A. Carapetyan, Director and Hänssler-Verlag, West Germany. All rights reserved. International copyright secured.

Ahime, dov'è 'l bel viso,
In cui solea tener nid' amore,
E dove ripost'era ogni mia speme,
Ch'ornav'il mondo di splendore,
Il mio caro thesoro, il sommo bene?
Oime, chi me 'l ritien', chi me lo cela?

O fortuna, o mort'ingorda,
Cieca spietat'e sorda,
Chi m'ha tolto 'l mio cor, chi me l'asconde?

Dov'è 'l ben mio che più non mi risponde?

Alas, where is the pretty face
in which love used to nest
and where rested my every hope,
adorning the world with splendor
My dear treasure, the highest good?
Alas, who keeps it from me, who hides it from me?

O luck, o greedy death,
blind, merciless and dumb.
Who has snatched away my heart, who hides it from me?

Where is my darling who answers me no more?

Adrian Willaert

Madrigal: *Aspro core e selvaggio e cruda voglia*

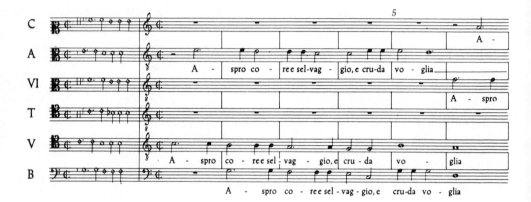

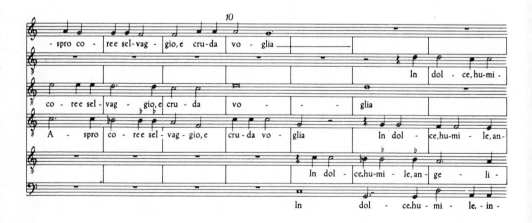

Willaert, *Musica nova* (Venice, 1559). This madrigal was probably composed in the mid-1540s. *Opera omnia*, ed. Hermann Zenck and Walter Gerstenberg, XIII (American Institute of Musicology, 1966), 54–60. Reprinted by permission of A. Carapetyan, Director and Hänssler-Verlag, West Germany. All rights reserved. International copyright secured.

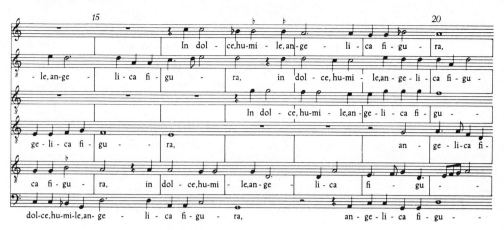

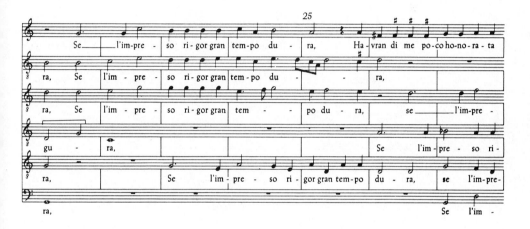

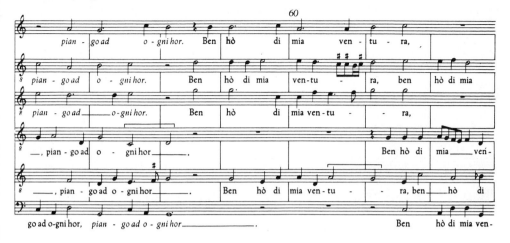

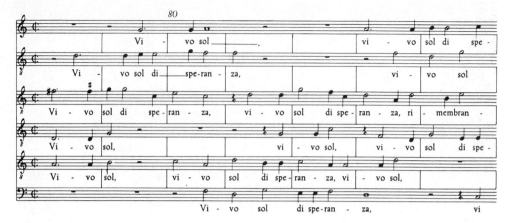

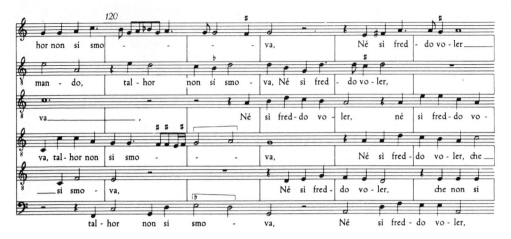

Aspro core e selvaggio, e cruda voglia
In dolce, umile, angelica figura,
Se l'impreso rigor gran tempo dura,
Avran di me poco honorata spoglia,
Che, quando nasce e mor fior, erba e foglia,

Quando è 'l dí chiaro e quando è notte oscura,

Piango ad ogni or. Ben ho di mia ventura,
Di madonna e d'Amore onde mi doglia.
Vivo sol di speranza, rimenbrando
Che poco umor già per continua prova
Consumar vidi marmi e pietre salde.

Non è sí duro cor che, lagrimando,
Pregando, amando, talhor non si smova,
Né sí freddo voler, che non si scalde.

FRANCESCO PETRARCA (1304–74)

Harsh heart and savage, and a cruel will
in a sweet, humble, angelic face,
if this adopted severity persist for long,
they will get from me spoils of little honor;
for when flower, grass, and leaf are born and
die,
when it is shining day and when it is dark
night,
I weep at every season. Well may I grieve,
for my luck, my lady and my love.
I live by hope alone, remembering
that by continuous drops
I have seen little liquid consume marble and
solid stones.
There is no heart so hard that weeping,
begging, loving sooner or later does not move,
nor so cold a resolve that it cannot be warmed.

CIPRIANO DE RORE (1516–65)
Madrigal: *Datemi pace, o duri miei pensieri*

Di Cipriano de Rore il secondo libro de madregali a quattro voci (Venice, 1557). *Opera omnia,* ed. Bernhard Meier, IV (American Institute of Musicology, 1969), 73–75. Reprinted by permission of A. Carapetyan, Director, and Hänssler-Verlag, West Germany. All rights reserved. International copyright secured.

20
no e'n su le por - te, Sen - za tro - var - mi den - tro al - tri guer- rie - ri?
no e'n su le por - te, Sen - za tro - var - mi den - tro al - tri guer - rie - ri?
no e'n su le por - te, Sen - za tro - var - mi den- - tro al-tri guer - rie - ri?
no e'n su le por - te, Sen - za tro - var - mi den - tro al-tri guer - rie - ri?
25
E tu, mio cor, e tu, mio cor, an - chor
E tu, mio cor, e tu, mio cor, an - chor
E tu, mio cor, an - chor se'
E tu, mio cor, e tu, mio cor, an - chor
30
35
se' pur qual e - - ri? Dis-le-al a me sol, che fie - re
se' pur qual e - - ri? Dis - le-al a me sol, che
pur qual e - ri? Dis - le -al a me sol, che
se' pur qual e - ri? Dis - le - al a me sol, che fie - re
40
scor - te Vai ri-cet-tan - do, fie - re scor-te Vai ri-cet-tan - do e sei fat - to con-
fie - re scor - te Vai ri-cet-tan-do, fie - re scor - te Vai ri - cet-tan - do e sei fat -
fie - re scor - te Vai ri-cet-tan-do, fie - re scor - te Vai ri-cet-tan - do
scor - te Vai ri-cet - tan - do, fie - re scor-te Vai ri-cet-tan - do
sor - te De' miei ne - mi - ci sì pron-ti e leg-gie - ri.
- to con - sor - te De' miei ne- mi - ci sì pron - ti e leg- gie - ri.
e sei fat - to con - sor - te De' miei ne - mi - ci sì pron -tie leg -
e sei fat - to con - sor - te De' miei ne -

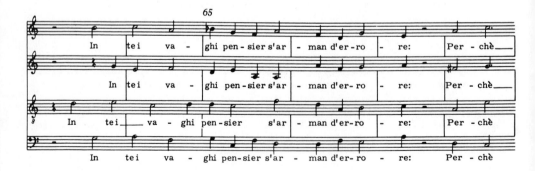

Datemi pace, o duri miei pensieri:
Non basta ben ch'Amor Fortuna e Morte
Mi fanno guerra intorno, e 'n su le porte,
Senza trovarmi dentro altri guerreri?
E tu, mio cor, ancor se' pur qual eri?
Disleal a me sol; che fere scorte

Vai ricettando e se' fatto consorte
De' miei nemici si pronti e leggieri.
In te i secreti suoi messaggi, Amore,
In te spiega Fortuna ogni sua pompa,
E Morte la memoria di quel colpo
Che l'avanzo di me convèn che rompa;

In te i vaghi pensier s'arman d'errore:

Per che d'ogni mio mal te solo incolpo.

Oh, give me peace, my jarring thoughts.
Is it not enough that Love, Fate, and Death
wage war all about me and at my very gates,
without finding other enemies within?
And you, my heart, are you still as you were?
Disloyal to me alone: for you harbor fierce spies
and have allied yourself
with my enemies, bold and brisk as they are.
In you Love reveals his secret messages,
in you Fate boasts all her triumphs,
and Death [awakens] the memory of that blow
which must surely destroy all that remains of me;
In you gentle thoughts arm themselves with falsity:
Wherefore I charge you alone guilty of all my ills.

F. PETRARCA

LUCA MARENZIO
Madrigal: *Solo e pensoso*

Luca Marenzio, *Il nono libro de madrigali a 5 voci* (Venice: Gardano, 1599), ed. Iain Fenlon, *Music and Patronage in Sixteenth-Century Mantua* (Cambridge: Cambridge University Press, 1982) 2:99–105.

Solo e pensoso i più deserti campi
Vò' misurando a passi tardi e lenti;
E gl'occhi porto, per fuggire, intenti,
Dove vestigio human l'arena stampi.
Altro scherno non trovo che mi scampi
Dal manifesto accorger de le genti;
Perchè negli atti d'allegrezza spenti
Di fuor si legge com'io dentro avampi:
Si ch'io mi credo homai che monti e piagge

E fiumi e selve sappian di che tempre
Sia la mia vita, ch'è celata altrui.
Ma pur sì aspre vie nè sì selvagge
Cercar non sò ch'Amor non venga sempre

Ragionando con meco, et io con lui.

FRANCESCO PETRARCA

Alone and pensive, the deserted fields,
I measure with deliberate and slow steps,
and my eyes I hold in readiness to flee
to a place marked by human footsteps.
Other defense I do not find that will save me
from the peering eyes of people.
Because when joy is gone from actions
my flame within can be read outside.
I've come to believe that mountains and
    beaches
and rivers and woods know of what fibers
is made my life, which is hidden from others.
Yet neither such rough nor wild paths
can I find where Love does not ever seek me
    out
to discuss with me and I with him.

CARLO GESUALDO (CA. 1560–1613)
Madrigal: *"Io parto" e non più dissi*

Gesualdo, *Madrigali a cinque voci; Libro sesto* (Gesualdo, 1611). *Sämtliche Madrigale für fünf Stimmen,* ed., Wilhelm Weismann, I, 29–32. © 1957 by Ugrino Verlag, Hamburg. Assigned to VEB Deutscher Verlag für Musik, Leipzig; Reprinted by permission.

"Io parto" e non più dissi che il dolore
Privò di vita il core.
Allor proruppe in pianto e dissi Clori
Con interroti omèi:
"Dunque a i dolori io resto. Ah, non fia mai

Ch'io non languisca in dolorosi lai."
Morto fui, vivo son che i spirti spenti

tornaro in vita a sì pietosi accenti.

"I depart" and said no more, for grief
robbed the heart of life.
Then he broke out in tears, and Clori said,
with interrupted cries of "Alas":
"Therefore, with my pains I remain. Ah, may
    I never
cease to languish in painful lays."
Dead I was, now am I alive, for the dead
    spirits
return to life at the sound of such pitiable ac-
    cents.

Thomas Weelkes (ca. 1575–1623)
Madrigal: *O Care, thou wilt despatch me*

Ed. Nigel Davison in John Wilbye et al., *Neun englische Madrigale zu 5 und 6 stimmen, Das Chorwerk* 132:37–44 (Wolfenbüttel: Moseler Verlag, 1983?). Reproduced by permission of Stainer & Bell, Ltd., London, England.

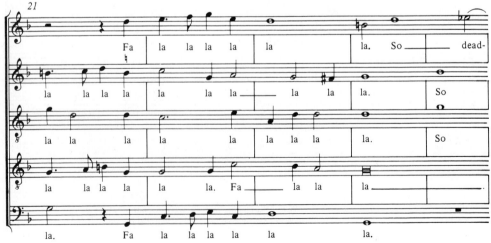

(Second part)

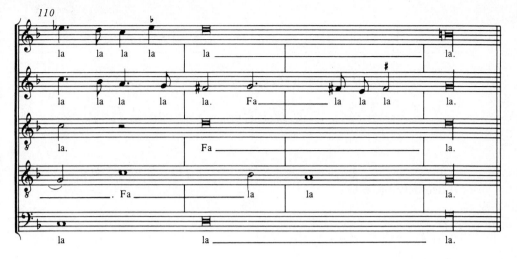

PIERRE ATTAINGNANT (D. 1552)*
Danseries a 4 Parties, Second Livre

a) Basse danse (No. 1)

*Editor of the collection. Note values reduced by half. Barlines through the entire brace mark the *quaternions* of the choreography; triple-time measures are set off by barlines through the staff; after every seventh minim of a *quaternion* a broken line appears. *Danseries a 4 parties, Second livre* (Paris, 1547), ed. Raymond Meylan (Paris: Heugel & Cie., c1969), pp. 1, 38–39. Used by permission of the Publisher, Theodore Presser Company, sole representative U.S.A.

b) Branle gay *Que je chatoulle ta fossette* (No. 36)

63

ROBERT MORTON (1440–75)
Chanson: *L'omme armé* for instruments

Jeanne Marix, *Les musiciens de la cour de Bourgogne au xvie siècle* (Paris: Éditions de L'Oiseau-lyre, 1937), p. 96. Reprinted by permission.

Luis Milán (ca. 1500–after 1561)
Fantasia XI for vihuela

Moderato e Rubato

Values halved. Milan, *Libro de musica de vihuela de mano, intitulado El Maestro,* ed. Charles Jacobs (University Park and London: The Pennsylvania State University Press, 1971), pp. 59–62. Reprinted by permission.

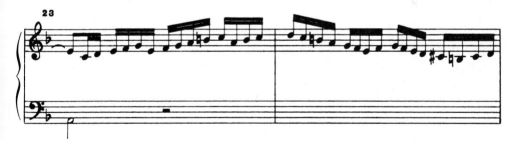

CHRISTOPHER TYE (CA. 1500–CA. 1572)
In nomine "Crye"

See no. 42 for the cantus firmus on which this is based. Christopher Tye, *The Instrumental Music,* ed. Robert W. Weidner (Madison: A–R Editions, 1967), pp. 34–38. Reprinted by permission.

*The rest is reduced by two-thirds.

**minim (quarter note in transcription) in the MS

*d in the MS

**G in the MS

66

GIULIO CACCINI (CA. 1550–1618)
Madrigal: *Perfidissimo volto*

Le nuove musiche (Florence, 1602). H. Wiley Hitchcock, editor, *Giulio Caccini, Le nuove musiche* (Madison: A–R Editions, Inc., 1970), p. 77–80.

Perfidissimo volto,
Ben l'usata bellezza in te si vede
Ma non l'usata fede.
Già mi parevi dir: Quest'amorose
Luci che dolcemente
Rivolgo a te, sì bell'e sì pietose

Prima vedrai tu spente,
Che sia spento il desio ch'a te le gira.
Ahi, che spento è 'l desio,
Ma non è spento quel per cui sospira
L'abbandonato core!
O volto troppo vago e troppo rio,
Perchè se perdi amore
Non perdi ancor' vaghezza
O non hai pari alla belta fermezza?

O, most perfidious face,
true, the usual beauty in you is seen,
but not the usual fidelity.
Once you seemed to say: "These amorous
eyes that sweetly
I turn towards you, so beautiful and so com-
            passionate —
first you will see these lights extinguished
before is spent the desire that they convey."
Alas, now spent is that desire,
but not spent is that for which sighs
the abandoned heart!
O face too lovely and too cruel,
why when you lose love,
do you not lose also loveliness,
and why do you not match beauty with con-
            stancy?

GIOVANNI BATTISTA GUARINI (1538–1612)

67

CLAUDIO MONTEVERDI (1567–1643)
Madrigal: *Cruda Amarilli*

Monteverdi, *Il quinto libro de madrigali a cinque voci* (Venice, 1606). *Tutte le opere di Claudio Monteverdi*, edited by G. Francesco Malipiero (© Copyright 1929 by Universal Edition A. G., Vienna), Vol. V, pp. 1–4. Copyright renewed. All rights reserved. Used by permission of European American Music Distributors Corp. Sole U.S. Agent for Universal Edition, Vienna.

1) Nell'originale:

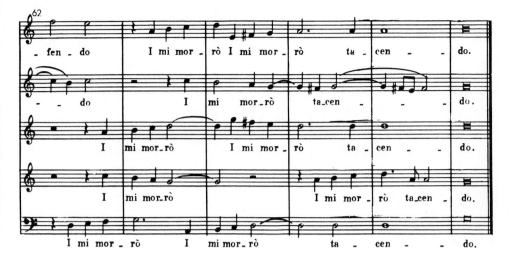

Cruda Amarilli che col nome ancora
D'amar, ahi lasso, amaramente insegni.
Amarilli del candido ligustro,
Più candida e più bella,
Ma dell'aspido sordo
E più sorda e più fera e più fugace.
Poi che col dir t'offendo
I mi morò tacendo.

G. B. GUARINI

Cruel Amaryllis, who with your name
to love, alas, bitterly you teach.
Amaryllis, more than the white privet
pure, and more beautiful,
but deafer than the asp,
and fiercer and more elusive.
Since telling I offend you,
I shall die in silence.

68

Claudio Monteverdi
Madrigal: *Ohimè dov' è il mio ben*
Romanesca a 2

Prima parte

Concerto, Settimo libro de madrigali a 1. 2. 3. 4. & 6. voci, con altri generi de canti (Venice, 1619). *Tutte le opere di Claudio Monteverdi*, edited by G. Francesco Malipiero (© Copyright 1929 by Universal Edition A. G., Vienna), Vol. VII, pp. 152–59. Copyright renewed. All rights reserved. Used by permission of European American Music Distributors Corp. Sole U.S. Agent for Universal Edition, Vienna.

Seconda parte

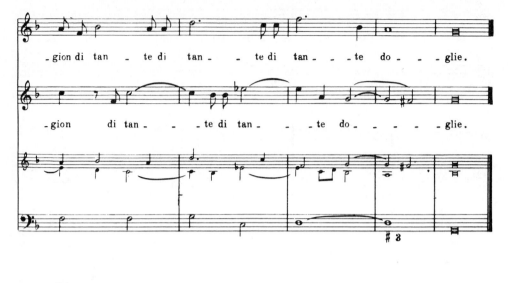

_gion di tan _ _ te di tan _ _ _ te di tan _ _ _ te do _ _ glie.

_gion   di tan _ _ _ te di tan _ _ _ te do _ _ _ _ glie.

Terza parte

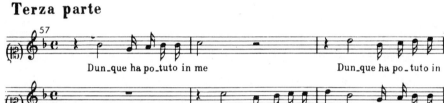

Dun_que ha po_tuto in me   Dun_que ha po_tuto in

Dun_que ha po_tuto in me Dun_que ha po_tuto in

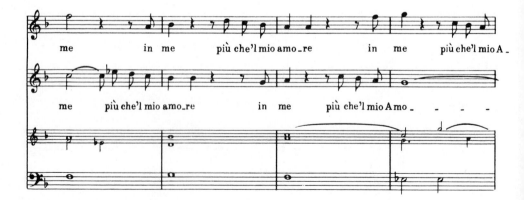

me   in me   più che'l mio amo_re   in   me   più che'l mio A _

me   più che'l mio amo_re   in   me   più che'l mio Amo _ _ _ _

Quarta e ultima parte

Che mi_ni_stro mi fai del_la mia mor_te la mia mor _ _ _ te.

Che mi_ni_stro mi fai del_la mia mor_te la mia mor _ _ '_ te.

Ohimè dov'è il mio ben, dov'è il mio core?
Chi m'asconde il mio ben e chi m'el toglie?

Dunque ha potuto sol desio d'honore
Darmi fera cagion di tante doglie.

Dunque ha potuto in me più che'l mio amore
Ambizios'e troppo lievi voglie.
Ahi sciocco mondo e cieco, ahi cruda sorte
Che ministro mi fai della mia morte.

BERNARDO TASSO (1493–1569)

Alas, where is my love, where is my heart?
Who conceals my treasure and who takes it away?

Thus desire for honor alone was capable
of giving me strong grounds for so many griefs.

Thus more power than my love had my
ambitious and too trifling aspirations.
Ah, stupid world, and blind; ah, cruel fate!
You make me executioner of my own death.

JOHN DOWLAND (1562–1626)
Air: *Flow my tears*

See Dowland's lute arrangement and the variations upon it by Byrd, Farnaby and Sweelinck in No. 98. *Second Booke of Songes* (London, 1600). *The English Lute Songs,* Series I, edited by Edmund H. Fellowes, revised by Thurston Dart, V–VI (London: Stainer & Bell, 1969), 4–6. Reprinted by permission.

- lorn.   Nev - er may my woes   be re - liev - ed,   Since pi -
- close.   From the high-est spire   of con - tent - ment   My for -

- ty is fled;   And tears   and sighs   and groans   my wea - ry
- tune is thrown;   And fear   and grief   and pain   for my de -

days,   my wea - ry days   Of   all joys   have de - priv - ed.
- serts,   for my de-serts   Are   my hopes, since hope is   gone.

Never may my woes be relieved,
  Since pity is fled;
And tears and sighs and groans my weary days
  Of all joys have deprived.

From the highest spire of contentment
  My fortune is thrown;
And fear and grief and pain for my deserts
  Are my hopes, since hope is gone.

Hark! you shadows that in darkness dwell,
  Learn to contemn light.
Happy, happy they that in hell
  Feel not the world's despite.

70

EMILIO DE' CAVALIERI (1550–1602)
Madrigal: *Dalle più alte sfere*
Intermedio I, 1589

(a) Sans barres de mesure. (b) En partition, avec barres de mesure.

This madrigal has also been attributed to Antonio Archilei. *Intermedii et concerti, fatti per la commedia rappresentata in Firenze nelle nozze del Serenissimo Don Ferdinando Medici, e Madama Christiana di Loreno, Gran Duchi di Toscana* (Venice, 1951). Edited by D. P. Walker, *Musique des intermèdes de "La Pellegrina"* (Paris: Éditions du Centre national de la recherche scientifique, 1963), pp. 2–8.

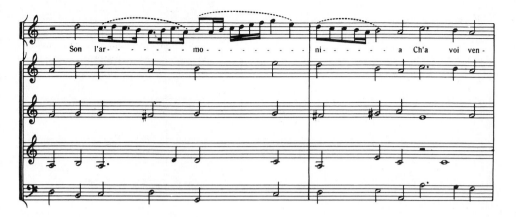

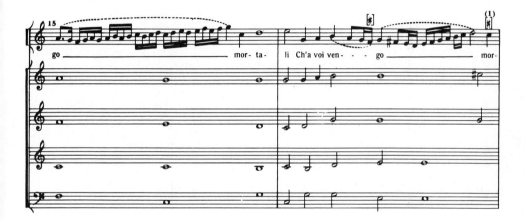

Son l'ar - - - - - - mo - - - - - - - ni - - - - - a Ch'a voi ven-

go _____ mor- ta- li Ch'a voi ven- - go _____ mor-

ta - li Po- scia che fin al ciel Po- scia che fi - no al ciel bat- ten- - do _____ l'a- li bat- ten- do

[sic]

l'a - - li batten - do   l'a - - - - - - - li   L'al - - ta fiam- ma L'al-ta _____

fiam- - ma N'ap- por - - - - - - ta   N'ap-por - - - - - - - - - - ta

Che mai si no - - bil _____ cop - - - pia'l sol _____ non

(1) &♭ 𝆕 𝅝. 𝅘𝅥 𝅘𝅥♯𝅘𝅥

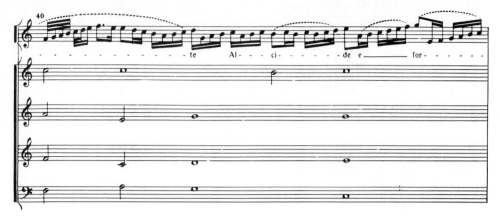

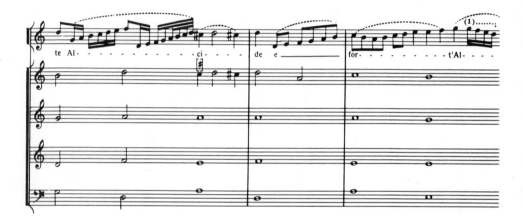

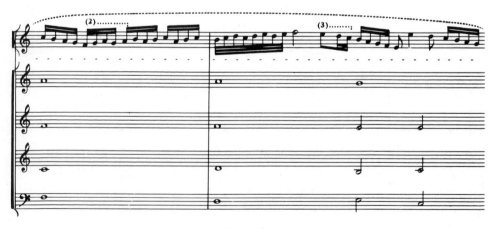

Dalle più alte sfere
Di celesti sirene amica scorta
Son l'armonia ch'a voi vengo mortali,
Poscia, che fino al ciel battendo l'ali
L'alta fiama n'apporta,
Che mai si nobil coppia 'l sol non vide
Qual voi nova Minerva e fort'Alcide.

GIOVANNI DE' BARDI (1534–1612)

From the highest spheres
of the heavenly sirens, a friendly escort,
I am Harmony, who comes to you mortals,
since even high in the sky, beating its wings,
lofty fame brought news
that never so noble a couple the sun did see
as you, new Minerva and brave Hercules.

71

JACOPO PERI (1561–1633)
Le musiche sopra l'Euridice

a) Prologo, La Tragedia: *Io, che d' alti sospir vaga e di pianti*

b) Tirsi: *Nel pur ardor della più bella stella*

Note values reduced by half. Original barring retained. Time signatures added by editor are in brackets; editorial accidentals are above staff. In the Prologue, the composer intended that rhythmic adjustments be made in the strophes. Peri, *Le musiche sopra l'Euridice* (Florence, 1601), pp. 2, 11–12, 14–17.

TIRSI

Nel pur ar-dor del-la più bel-la stel-la   Au-rea fa-cel-la
Lie-to I-me-neo d'al-ta dol-cez-za un nem-bo   Tra-boc-ca in grem-bo a

di bel foc' ac-cen-di,   E qui di-scen-di   su l'au-ra-te piu-me,
for-tu-na-ti a-man-ti   E tra bei can-ti   di so-a-vi a mo-ri

Gio-con-do Nu-me, E di ce-le-ste fiam-ma L'a-ni-me in-fiam-ma.
Sve-glia nei co-ri u-na dol-ce au-ra un ri-so Di Pa-ra-di-so.

c) Dafne: *Per quel vago boschetto*
    Arcetro: *Chi narri, ohimè*
    Orfeo, *Non piango e non sospiro*

ta - va, al mor-mo-rar dell' on - da. Ma la bel - la Eu-ri - di - ce Mo-vea dan-zan-do il

10 11 10

piè sul ver - de pra - to, Quand'ahi ria sor - te a - cer - ba! An-gue cru-do, e spie -

ta - to, Che ce-la - to gia-cea tra' fio - ri e l'er - ba, Pun - se-le il piè con si ma -

li - gno den - te, Ch'im-pa-li - dì re-pen - te Co-me rag-gio di sol che nu - be a

dom - bri E dal pro-fon-do co - re Con un so-spir mor-ta-le Si spa-ven-to-so ohi-mè so-spin-se

fuo - re. Che, qua-si a-ves - se l'a - le, Giun-se o-gni Nin - fa al do-lo-ro - so suo - no, Et

el - la in ab-ban-do - no Tut-ta la-scios-si all' or nel-l'al-trui brac-cia. Spar-gea il bel vol -

to, e le do-ra - te chio-me Un su-dor viè più fred-d'as-sai __ che giac - cio. In - di s'u-dio'l tuo

no-me Tra le lab-bra so-nar fred-d'e'tre-man-ti E, vol-ti gl'oc-chi al cie-lo, Sco-lo -

ri-to il bel vol-to, e' bei sem-bian-ti, Res-tò tan - ta bel-lez-za im-mo-bil gie

lo. Che nar - ri, ohi - mè, che sen - to? Mi - se - ra Nin - fa, e

più mi - se-ro a-man - te, Spet - ta - col di mi - se - ria e di tor - men - to! Non

pian - go e non sos-pi - ro, O mia ca - ra Eu - ri-di - ce, Ché sos-pi - rar,___

ché la-cri-mar non pos - so. Ca-da - ve-ro in-fe-li - ce, O___ mio co - re o mia

spe - me, o pa-ce, o vi - ta! Ohi - mè, chi___ mi t'ha tol - to, Chi mi t'ha

tol - to, o - hi - mè!___ do - ve sei gi - ta?

To - sto ve - drai___ ch'in va - no Non chia - ma - sti mo - ren - do il___ tuo con - sor - te. Non

son, non son lon - ta - no: Io ven - go, o ca - ra vi - ta, o ca - ra mor - te

PROLOGUE: TRAGEDY

Io, che d'alti sospir vaga e di pianti,	I, who with deep sighs and tears am smitten,
Spars' or di doglia, hor di minaccie il volto,	my face, covered now with grief, now with menace,
Fei negl'ampi teatri al popol folto	once in ample theatres crowded with people
Scolorir di pietà volti e sembianti.	made their faces turn pale with pity.
Non sangue sparso d'innocenti vene,	Not of blood spilled from innocent veins,
Non ciglia spente di tiranno insano,	nor of eyes put out by an insane tyrant,
Spettacolo infelice al guardo umano,	but a spectacle unhappy to the human sight,
Canto su meste e lagrimose scene.	do I sing on this sad and tearful stage.
Lungi via, lungi pur da' regi tetti	Stay far from under this royal roof,
Simulacri funesti, ombre d'affanni:	dismal images, shadows of anguish.
Ecco i mesti coturni e i foschi panni	Behold, the gloomy buskins and the dark rags
Cangio, e desto ne i cor più dolci affetti.	I transform, and awaken in the hearts sweeter affections.
Hor s'avverràche le cangiate forme	Now, if it should happen that the changed forms
Non senza alto stupor la terra ammiri.	not without great amazement the world should admire,

Tal ch'ogni alma gentil ch'Apollo inspiri
Del mio novo cammin calpesti l'orme,

so that every gentle genius that Apollo inspires
takes up the tracks, of my new path,

Vostro, Regina, fia cotanto alloro,
Qual forse anco non colse Atene, o Roma,

Yours, Queen, will be so much laurel
that perhaps not even Athens or Rome won
more,

Fregio non vil su l'onorata chioma,
Fronda Febea fra due corone d'oro.

no mean ornament on the honored head,
a leafy branch of Phoebus between two
crowns.

Tal per voi torno, e con sereno aspetto

Thus for you I return, and with a serene countenance

Ne' reali Imenei m'adorno anch'io,
E su corde più liete il canto mio
Tempro, al nobile cor dolce diletto.

at this royal wedding I too adorn myself,
and with happier notes my song
I temper, for the noble heart's sweet delight.

Mentre Senna real prepara intanto
Alto diadema, onde il bel crin si fregi

Meanwhile the royal Seine prepares
a lofty diadem with which the beautiful hair to
crown

E i manti e' seggi de gl'antichi regi,
Del Tracio Orfeo date l'orecchie al canto.

and the cloaks and thrones of ancient kings;
to the song of the Thracian Orpheus, lend
your ears.

TIRSI

Nel pur ardor della più bella stella
Aurea facella di bel foc'accendi,
E qui discendi su l'aurate piume,
Giocondo Nume, e de celeste fiamma
L'anime infiamma.

With the pure flame of the brightest star
light the golden torch with beautiful fire
and here descend on aurous wings,
o happy God, and with celestial fire
the souls inflame.

TIRSI

Lieto Imeneo d'alta dolcezza un nembo

Happy Hymen, let your shower of lofty
sweetness

Trabocca in grembo a' fortunati amanti

overflow into the breasts of the fortunate
lovers

E tra bei canti di soavi amori
Sveglia nei cori una dolce aura, un riso
Di Paradiso.

and, amidst pretty songs of delightful loves,
stir in their hearts a gentle breeze, a smile
of Paradise.

DAFNE

Per quel vago boschetto,
Ove, rigando i fiori,
Lento trascorre il fonte degl'allori,
Prendea dolce diletto
Con le compagne sue la bella sposa,
Chi violetta o rosa
Per far ghirland' al crine
Togliea dal prato o dall'acute spine,
E qual posand' il fianco
Su la fiorita sponda
Dolce cantava al mormorar dell 'onda;
Ma la bella Euridice

In the beautiful thicket,
where, watering the flowers,
slowly passing the fount of the laurel,
she took sweet delight
with her companions—the beautiful bride—
as some picked violets, others, roses,
to make garlands for their hair,
in the meadow or among the sharp thorns.
Another, lying on her side
on the flowered bank,
sang sweetly to the murmur of the waves.
But the lovely Eurydice

Movea danzando il piè sul verde prato

Quand'ahi ria sorte acerba,
Angue crudo e spietato
Che celato giacea tra fiori e l'erba
Punsele il piè con si maligno dente,
Ch'impalidì repente
Come raggio di sol che nube adombri.
E dal profondo core,
Con un sospir mortale,
Si spaventoso ohimè sospinse fuore,
Che, quasi avesse l'ale,
Giunse ogni Ninfa al doloroso suono.
Et ella in abbandono
Tutta lasciossi all'or nell'altrui braccia.
Spargea il bel volto e le dorate chiome

Un sudor viè più fredd'assai che giaccio.
Indi s'udio 'l tuo nome
Tra le labbra sonar fredd'e' tremanti
E volti gl'occhi al cielo,
Scolorito il bel volto e' bei sembianti,
Restò tanta bellezza immobil gielo.

was moving, with dancing steps, her feet on
the green grass
when—o bitter, angry fate!
a snake, cruel and merciless,
that lay hidden among flowers and grass
bit her foot with such an evil tooth
that she suddenly became pale
like a ray of sunshine that a cloud darkens.
And from the depths of her heart,
a mortal sigh,
so frightful, alas, flew forth,
almost as if it had wings;
every nymph rushed to the painful sound.
And she, fainting,
let herself fall in another's arms.
Then spread over her beautiful face and her
golden tresses
a sweat colder by far than ice.
And then was heard your name, sounding
between her lips, cold and trembling,
and her eyes turned to heaven,
her beautiful face and mien discolored,
this great beauty was transformed to motion-
less ice.

ARCETRO

Che narri, ohimè, che sento?
Misera Ninfa, e più misero amante,
Spettacol di miseria e di tormento!

What do you relate, alas, what do I hear?
Wretched nymph, and more unhappy lover,
spectacle of sorrow and of torment!

ORFEO

Non piango e non sospiro,
O mia cara Euridice,
Ché sospirar, ché lacrimar non posso.
Cadavero infelice,
O mio core, o mia speme, o pace, o vita!
Ohimè, chi mi t'ha tolto,
Chi mi t'ha tolto, ohimè! dove sei gita?

Tosto vedrai ch'in vano
Non chiamasti morendo il tuo consorte.
Non son, non son lontano:
Io vengo, o cara vita, o cara morte.

I do not weep, nor do I sigh,
o my dear Eurydice,
for I am unable to sigh, to weep.
Unhappy corpse,
o my heart, o my hope, o peace, o life!
, Alas, who has taken you from me?
Who has taken you away, alas? Where have
you gone?
Soon you will see then not in vain
did you, dying, call your spouse.
I am not far away:
I come, o dear life, o dear death.

OTTAVIO RINUCCINI (1562–1621)

72

Claudio Monteverdi
L'Orfeo, Favola in musica

a) Prologo, La Musica: *Dal mio Permesso amato a voi ne vegno*

Dal mio permesso a_ma_to a voi ne ve_gno in_cli_ti e_roi san_gue gen_til de Re_gi di cui nar_ra la fa_ma ec_cel_si pre_gi ne giun_ge al ver perch'è trop_p'al_to il se___gno.

Correction to the score: p. 343, m. 31, instead of C, the bass should be C-sharp, as it is in the 1609 and 1615 editions. *Tutte le opere di Claudio Monteverdi,* edited by G. Francesco Malipiero (© Copyright 1929 by Universal Edition A. G., Vienna). Vol. XI, 3–18, 48–50, 59–65. Copyright renewed. All rights reserved. Used by permission of European American Music Distributors Corp. Sole U.S. Agent for Universal Edition, Vienna.

Ritornello

Io la mu_si_ca son ch'ai dol_ci ac_cen_ _ _ti so far tranquil_lo

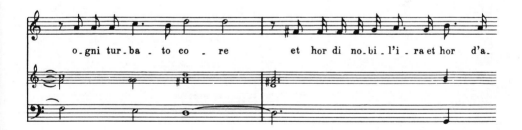

o_gni tur_ba _ to co _ re et hor di no_bi_l'i _ ra et hor d'a_

_mo_re pos_ _ _ _s'in_fiammar le più ge_la_ _ te men _ ti.

Ritornello

Io su ce_te_ra d'or cantan_do so _ glio mor_tal o_rec_chio

lu_sin_gar ta_l'ho _ ra e in que_sta gui _ sa a l'ar_mo_

_nia so_no_ra de la li _ ra del ciel più l'al _ me in_vo_glio.

Ritornello

Quin_ci a dir_vi d'Orfeo de_sio mi spro___na, d'Or_feo che tras_se

al suo can_tar le fe _ re e ser_vo fe' l'In_fer_no a sue pre_

_ghie _ re Glo _ ria immortal di Pin_do e d'E_li_co _ na.

Ritornello

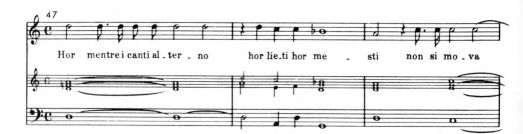

Hor mentre i canti al _ ter _ no   hor lie_ti hor me _ sti   non si mo _ va

Au _ gel _ lin   fra   que _ ste pian _ te   ne s'o _ da

in que_ste ri _ ve on _ da so _ nan _ te   et   o _ gni au_

_ret _ ta   in suo cam _ min   s'ar_re _   _ sti.

Ritornello

b) Act II, Orfeo: *Vi ricorda o boschi ombrosi* (excerpt)

Ritornello

ORFEO

c) Act II, Messagera: *In un fiorito prato*
   Orfeo: *Tu se' morta*
   Choro: *Ahi caso acerbo*

MESSAG.

In un fio-ri-to pra-to con

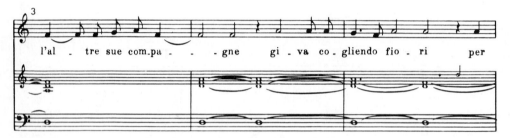

l'al - tre sue com-pa - - gne gi - va co-gliendo fio-ri per

far - ne u-na ghirlan-da a a le sue chio-me, quand'an-gue in-si-dio-so ch'e-

- ra fra l'erbe asco-so, le pun-se un piè con ve-le-no-so den-te.

Ed ec _ co imman _ ti _ nente sco _ lo _ rir _ si il bel vi _ so

e nei suoi lumi sparir que lam _ pi ond'ella al sol fea scor _ no al _

_ l'hor noi tut _ te sbi _ got _ ti _ te e me _ ste le fummo intor _ no ri _ chia _

_ mar tentando li spir_ti in lei smarri_ti con l'onda fresca e con possen_ti carmi, ma

nul_la val_sè ahi las _ sa ch'el_la i langui_di lu _ mi alquan_to apren_

può do_ler_si; Ahi ben havrebbe un cor di Tigre o d'Orsa chi non sentis_se

del tuo mal pie_ta_te, pri_vo d'ogni tuo ben mi_se_ro a_man_te.

ORFEO

Tu se' mor_ta se' mor_ta mia vi_

Un organo di legno e un chitarone

ta ed io respi _ro, tu se' da me par_ti_ta,

se' da me par_ti_ta per mai più, mai più non torna_re ed io ri_man_

_go, no, no, che se i ver_si al_cu_na co_sa pon_no,

n'andrò si_cu_ro a più profon_di a_bis_si e in_te_ne_ri_to il

cor del Re de l'om_bre me_co trar_rot_ti a ri_ve_der le

stel_le, O se ciò ne_ghe_rammi em_pio de_sti_no,

ri_marrò te_co in compagnia di mor_te a dio ter_ra

a dio cie _ lo e So _ le, a Di _ o.

Ahi ca _ so a _ cer _ bo, Ahi fat'em _ pio e cru _ de _ le, Ahi stel_le ingiu_rio_

Ahi ca _ so a _ cer _ bo, Ahi fat'empio e cru_de_ le, Ahi stel_le ingiu_rio_

Ahi ca _ so a _ cer _ bo, Ahi fa _ t'em_pio e cru _ de _ le, Ahi stel_le ingiu_rio_

Ahi ca _ so a _ cer _ bo, Ahi fa _ t'em _ pio e cru_de_ le, Ahi stel_le ingiu_rio_

Ahi ca _ so a _ cer _ bo, Ahi fa _ t'em _ pio e cru_de _ le, Ahi stel_le ingiu_rio_

_ se ahi cie _ lo a _ va _ ro. Non si fidi huom mor _ ta _ le

_ se ah cie _ lo a va _ ro. Non si fi _ di huom mor _ ta _ le

_ se ahi ciel a _ va _ _ ro. Non si fi _ di huom mor _ ta _ le

_ se ahi ciel _ a _ va _ ro. Non si fi _ di huom mor _ ta _ le Di ben ca_

_ se ahi cie _ lo a _ va _ _ ro. Non si fi _ di huom mor _ ta _ le

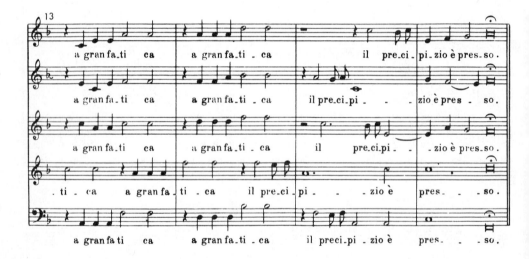

MUSIC

Dal mio Permesso amato a voi ne vegno,	From my beloved Permessus I come to you,
Incliti Eroi, sangue gentil de' Regi	Illustrious heroes, noble blood of kings,
Di cui narra la Fama eccelsi pregi,	of whom Fame relates their lofty worth,
Ne giunge al ver perch'è tropp'alto il segno.	yet falls short of the truth because the standard is too high.
Io la Musica son, ch'ai dolci accenti	I am Music, who, through sweet accents
So far tranquillo ogni turbato core,	know how to quiet every troubled heart,
Et hor di nobil' ira et hor d'amore	now with noble ire and now with love,
Poss' infiammar le più gelate menti.	I can inflame the most frozen spirits.

Io su cetera d'òr cantando soglio
Mortal orecchio lusingar tal'hora
E in questa guisa a l'armonia sonora
De la lira del ciel più l'alme invoglio.

I, on kithara of gold am used to singing,
charming mortal ears on occasion,
and in this guise to the sonorous harmony
of the heavenly lyre, the spirits beguile.

Quinci a dirvi d'Orfeo desio mi sprona,

Hence to tell you of Orpheus the desire spurs
        me:

D'Orfeo che trasse al suo cantar le fere

of Orpheus, who with his singing attracted the
        beasts,

E servo fè l'Inferno a sue preghiere
Gloria immortal di Pindo e d'Elicona.

and made a servant of Hell with his pleas,
immortal glory of Pindus and Helicon.

Hor mentre i canti alterno hor lieti, hor mesti,
Non si mova augellin fra queste piante,
Ne s'oda in queste rive onda sonante,

Now while I alternate happy and sad songs,
not a bird moves among these trees,
nor is heard on these shores a resounding
        wave,

Et ogni auretta in suo cammin s'arresti.

and every little breeze arrests its course.

ORPHEUS

Vi ricorda, o boschi ombrosi,
de' miei lungh' aspri tormenti,
quando i sassi ai miei lamenti
rispondean, fatti pietosi?

Do you recall, o shady woods,
my long, bitter torments,
when the stones to my laments
replied, pitiable deeds?

MESSENGER

In un fiorito prato
Con l'altre sue compagne
Giva cogliendo fiori
Per farne una ghirlanda a le sue chiome,
Quand'angue insidioso,
Ch'era fra l'erbe ascoso,
Le punse un piè con velenoso dente:
Ed ecco immantinente
Scolorirsi il bel viso e nei suoi lumi
Sparir que lampi, ond'ella al sol fea scorno.
All'hor noi tutte sbigottite e meste
Le fummo intorno, richiamar tentando
Li spirti in lei smarriti
Con l'onda fresca e con possenti carmi;
Ma nulla valse, ahi lassa!
Ch'ella i languidi lumi alquanto aprendo,
E te chiamando Orfeo,
Dopo un grave sospiro
Spirò fra queste braccia, ed io rimasi
Piena il cor di pietade e di spavento.

In a flowered meadow
with her companions
she was going about gathering flowers
to make a garland for her hair,
when a treacherous serpent
that was hidden in the grass
bit her foot with venemous tooth:
Then at once
her face became pale, and in her eyes
those lamps that vied with the sun grew dim.
Then we all, frightened and sad,
gathered around calling, tempting
the spirits that were smothered in her
with fresh water and powerful songs.
But nothing helped, alas,
for she, opening her languid eyes slightly,
called to you, Orpheus,
and, after a deep sigh,
expired in these arms, and I remained
with heart full of pity and terror.

SHEPHERD

Ahi caso acerbo, ahi fat' empio e crudele!
Ahi stelle ingiuriose, ahi cielo avaro!

Ah, bitter event, ah, wicked fate and cruel!
Ah, malicious stars, ah, greedy heavens!

A l'amara novella
rassembra l'infelice un muto sasso,

The bitter news
has turned the unfortunate one into a mute
        stone;

che per troppo dolor non può dolersi.

from too much pain, he can feel no pain.

Ahi ben havrebbe un cor di Tigre o d'Orsa
Chi non sentisse del tuo mal pietate,
Privo d'ogni tuo ben, misero amante!

Ah, he must have the heart of a tiger or a bear
who did not feel pity for your loss,
as you are bereft of your dear one, wretched
    lover.

ORPHEUS

Tu se' morta, mia vita, ed io respiro?
Tu se' da me partita
Per mai più non tornare, ed io rimango?
No, che se i versi alcuna cosa ponno,
N'andrò sicuro a' più profondi abissi,
E intenerito il cor del Re de l'Ombre

You are dead, my life, and I still breathe?
You have departed from me,
never to return, and I remain?
No, for if verses have any power
I shall go safely to the most profound abyss,
and having softened the heart of the King of
    the Shades

Meco trarrotti a riveder le stelle,

I shall bring you back to see the stars once
    again,

O se ciò negherammi empio destino
Rimarrò teco in compagnia di morte,

and if this is denied me by wicked fate,
I shall remain with you in the company of
    death.

A dio terra, a dio cielo, e sole, a Dio.

Farewell earth, farewell sky and sun, farewell.

CHORUS

Ahi caso acerbo, ahi fat'empio e crudele!
Ahi stelle ingiuriose, ahi cielo avaro!
Non si fidi huom mortale
Di ben caduco e frale
Che tosto fugge, e spesso
A gran salita il precipizio è presso.

Ah, bitter event, ah, wicked fate and cruel!
Ah, malicious stars, ah greedy heavens!
Trust not, mortal man,
in goods fleeting and frail,
for they easily slip away and after a great as-
    cent the precipice is near.

ALESSANDRO STRIGGIO (1573–1630)

73

Claudio Monteverdi
L'Incoronazione di Poppea,
Drama in Musica (1642): Act I, Scene 3

255 POPPEA

Signor, signor deh, nonparti _ re sostien che queste braccia ti circondino il

260

col _ lo co _ me le tue bel lez _ ze cir _ con _ da _ no il cor mi _ o.

264 POPPEA

Non par_tir, non partir, Si _

NERONE

Poppe _ a la _ sia ch'io par _ ta.

Tutte le opere di Claudio Monteverdi, edited by G. Francesco Malipiero (© Copyright 1929 by Universal Edition A. G., Vienna), Vol. XIII, pp. 29–35. Copyright renewed. All rights reserved. Used by permission of European American Music Distributors Corp. Sole U.S. Agent for Universal Edition, Vienna.

POPPEA

_gnor deh non parti _ re,   ap _ pe _ na spunta l'al _ ba   e tu che se _ i l'incarna _ to mio

so _ le   la mia pal _ pa _ bil lu _ ce,   e l'amo _ ro _ so dì.   de la mia vi _ ta

vuoi si repen _ te far   da   me   da me   da   me da me par _ ti _   _ ta?

Deh   non dir   di par _ tir   che di vo _ ce sia _ ma _ rau n so _ lo accen _ to A _

_ hi pe _ rir   A _ hi   spi _ rar   quest'al _ ma io sen _   to.

304 POPPEA

mi_o benmi_o,   Vanne vanne ben mi_o ben mi_o, van _ ne ben mi _ _ _ o.

310 Ritornello

320 NERONE

In un so_spir,   sospir che vien   dal pro _ fon _ do del cor   In un so_

324

_spir,   sospir che vien   sospir che vien   dal pro _ fon _ do del   cor   in_cludo un

329

ba _ cio   o   ca _ ra, ca _ ra et   un   a Di _ _ o   Si ri_ve_

Signor, deh non partire,
Sostien, che queste braccia
Ti circondino il collo,
Come le tue bellezze
Circondano il cor mio.

Poppea, lascia ch'io parta.

Nor partir, Signor, deh non partire
Appena spunta l'alba, et tu che sei

L'incarnato mio Sole,
La mia palpabil luce,
E l'amoroso dì de la mia vita,
Vuoi sì repente far da me partita!

Deh non dir
Di partir,
Che di voce sì amara a un solo accento
Ahi, perir, ahi spirar quest'alma io sento.

La nobiltà de nascimenti tuoi
Non permette che Roma
Sappia che siamo uniti.
In sin ch'Ottavia non riman' esclusa
Col repudio da me: Vanne, ben mio;
In un sospir, che vien
Dal profondo del cor
Includo un bacio, o cara et un' a Dio,
Si rivedrem ben tosto, Idolo mio.

Signor, sempre mi vedi,
Anzi mai non mi vedi.
Perchè s'è ver, che nel tuo cor io sia
Entr' al tuo sen celata
Non posso da' tuoi lumi esser mirata.

POPPEA
    Sir, please don't go.
    Allow these arms
    to encircle your neck,
    as your beauty
    encircles my heart.

NERO
    Poppea, let me go.

POPPEA
    Don't leave, Sir, please don't go.
    The dawn is barely breaking, and you, who
        are
    my incarnated Sun,
    my light made palpable,
    the loving day of my life,
    want to part from me so quickly.

    Please, don't say
    that you're leaving.
    It is such a bitter word that from one hint of it,
    ah, I feel my soul dying, expiring.

NERO
    The nobility of your birth
    does not permit that Rome
    should know that we are together,
    until Ottavia is set aside,
    repudiated by me. Go, my dear.
    within a sigh that rises
    from the depths of my heart
    I enclose a kiss, dearest, and a farewell.
    We shall see each other soon, my idol.

POPPEA
    My lord, you see me constantly;
    rather, you never see me.
    Because, if it's true that I am in your heart,
    hidden in your breast,
    I cannot by your eyes be viewed.

NERO

Adorati miei rai,	My adored rays,
Deh restate homai	please stay, then;
Rimanti, o mia Poppea,	remain, O my Poppea,
Cor, vezzo, e luce mia.	my heart, my charm, my light.

POPPEA

Deh non dir. . . .   Please don't say . . .

NERO

Non temer, tu stai meco a tutte l'hore,	Do not fear; stay with me for all time,
Splendor negl'occhi, e deità nel core.	splendor of my eyes, goddess of my heart.

GIOVANNI FRANCESCO BUSENELLO

(1598–1659)

74

Marc' Antonio Cesti (1623–69)
Orontea (ca. 1649): Act II, Scene 17, Aria, *Intorno all' idol mio*

Edited by William Holmes (Wellesley: Wellesley Edition, No. 11, 1973), pp. 158–62.

Au — re__, au — re__ so — a — vi e gra ——— te_____, E__ nel·le guan—ce e—

—let—te Ba — cia —— te –lo per me__, cor — te — si, cor — te — si au — ret ——— te_

_____. E nel·le guan—ce e—let—te Ba — cia ——— te –lo per me__, ba — cia —— te–lo per

me___, cor — te — si, cor — te — si au — ret ——— te____.

Al mio ben__ che ri — po—sa Su l'a ——— li_ del ——— la

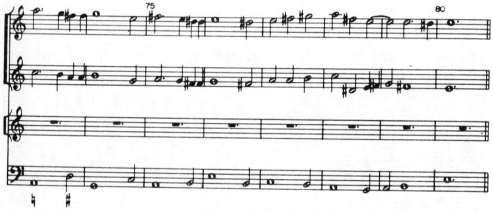

Intorno all'idol mio	Around my idol
Spirate, pur spirate	breathe, just breathe,
Aure soavi e grate	breezes sweet and pleasant,
E nelle guance elette	and on the favored cheeks
Baciatelo per me, cortesi aurette.	kiss him for me, gentle breezes.
Al mio ben che riposa	To my darling, who sleeps
Su l'ali della quiete	on the wings of calm,
Grati sogni assistete,	happy dreams induce;
E'l mio racchiuso ardore	and my covert ardor
Svelateli per me, larve d'amore.	unveil to him, phantoms of love.

GIACINTO ANDREA CICOGNINI
(1606–before 1651)

75

JEAN-BAPTISTE LULLY (1632–87)
Armide, Tragédie en 5 actes
et un prologue (1686)

a) Ouverture

Edited by Robert Eitner, *Publikationen älterer praktischer und theoretischer Musikwerke,* Vol. XIV (Leipzig: Breitkopf & Härtel, 1885), 1–3, 100–4.

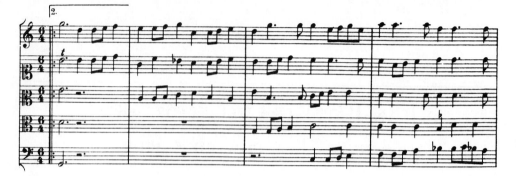

b) Act II, Scene 5, Armide: *Enfin il est en ma puissance*

Armide. *(tenent un dard à la main.)*

En - fin il est en ma puis-san - ce. Ce fa-tal en-ne - mi, ce su-per - be vain -

queur. La char-me du som - meil -le liv -re à ma ven-gean - ce; je vais per-cer son in-vin-ci - ble

(*Armide*

coeur. Par lui tous mes cap-tifs sont sor-tis d'es-cla - va-ge; qu'il é-prou-ve tou-te ma ra - ge. Quel

32 *va pour frapper Renaud et ne peut exécuter le dessein qu'elle a de lui òter la vie.*)

trou-ble me sai-sit? qui me fait hé -si - ter? qu'est-ce qu'en sa fa - veur la pi- tié me veut

di - re? Frap-pons ciel! qui peut m'ar-ré - ter? A-che vons… je fré-

40

mis! ven-geons-nous… je sou - pi - re! Est-ce ain-si que je dois me ven-ger au-jour-

d'hui! Ma co-lè-re s'é - teint quand j'ap-pro-che de lui. Plus je le voi, plus ma ven-geance est

vai - ne; mon bras trem-blant se re-fuse á ma hai - ne. Ah!_____ quel - le cru-au-

té de lui ra - vir le jour! A ce jeu-ne hé - ros tout cè - de sur la ter - re. Qui croi-

rait qu'il fut ne seu-le-ment pour la guer - re? Il sem-ble e - tre fait pour l'a - mour.

Ne puis - je me ven - ger à moins qu'il ne pé - ris - se? Hé! ne suf-fit - il

pas que l'a-mour le pu - nis - se? Puis - qu'il n'a pu trou - ver mes yeux as - sez char-

mants, qu'il m'aime au moins par mes en-chan-te - ments, que s'il se peut, je le ha-

ïs - se.

Ve-nez, ve-

nez, se-con-der mes dé-sirs, dé-mons, trans-for-mez vous en d'ai-ma-bles zé-phirs; ve-nez, ve-

phirs. Je cède a ce vain-queur la pi-tié me sur-mon-te, ca-chez ma foi-

ARMIDE

Enfin il est en ma puissance,	Finally he is in my power,
Ce fatal ennemi ce superbe vainqueur.	this fatal enemy, this superb warrior.
Le charme du sommeille livre à ma vengeance;	The charm of sleep delivers him to my vengeance;
Je vais percer son invincible coeur.	I will pierce his invincible heart.
Par lui tous mes captifs sont sortis d'esclavage;	Through him all my captives have escaped from slavery.
Qu'il éprouve toute ma rage.	Let him feel all my anger.
Quel trouble me saisit? qui me fait hésiter?	What fear grips me? what makes me hesitate?
Qu'est-ce qu'en sa faveur le pitié me veut dire?	What in his favor does pity want to tell me?
Frappons . . . Ciel! qui peut m'arrêter?	Let us strike . . . Heavens! Who can stop me?
Achevons . . . je frémis! vengeons – nous . . . je soupire!	Let us get on with it . . . I tremble! Let us avenge . . . I sigh!
Est-ce ainsi que je dois me venger aujourd'hui?	Is it thus that I must avenge myself today?
Ma colère s'éteint quand j'approche de lui.	My rage is extinguished when I approach him.
Plus je le voi, plus ma vengeance est vaine;	The more I see of him, the more my vengeance is ineffectual.
Mon bras tremblant se refuse à ma haine.	My trembling arm denies my hate.
Ah! quelle cruauté de lui ravir le jour!	Ah! What cruelty, to rob him of the light of day!

A ce jeune héros tout cède sur la terre.

Qui croirait qu'il fut ne seulement pour la
  guerre?
Il semble être fait pour l'Amour.
Ne puis – je me venger à moins qu'il ne
  périsse?
Hé! ne suffit-il pas que l'amour le punisse?

Puisqu'il n'a pu trouver mes yeux assez char-
  mants,
Qu'il m'aime au moins par mes enchante-
  ments,
Que, s'il se peut, je le haïsse.
Venez, venez, seconder mes désirs,
Démons, transformez – vous en d'aimables
  zéphirs.
Je cède à ce vainqueur, la pitié me surmonte.

Cachez ma foiblesse et ma honte
Dans les plus reculés déserts.
Volez, volez, conduisez – nous au bout de
  l'univers.

To this young hero everything on earth surren-
  ders.

Who would believe that he was born only for
  war?
He seems to be made for love.
Could I not avenge myself unless he dies?

Oh, is it not enough that Love should punish
  him?
Since he could not find my eyes charming
  enough,
let him love me at least through my sorcery,

so that, if it's possible, I may hate him.
Come, come support my desires,
demons; transform yourselves into friendly
  zephyrs.
I give in to this conqueror; pity overwhelms
  me.
Conceal my weakness and my shame
in the most remote desert.
Fly, fly, lead us to the end of the universe.

PHILIPPE QUINAULT (1635–88)

76

HENRY PURCELL (1659–95)
The Fairy Queen, An Opera in Five Acts
(1692)

a) *Thus the ever grateful Spring*

Text by Elkanah Settle (?) from Shakespeare's *Midsummer Night's Dream*. Reprinted by Broude Bros. (New York, 19--), pp. 134–36, 150–56, 179–82.

b) *Hark! The ech'ing air*

sings,   Hark!   hark! the ech-'ing air a tri - - - - umph sings

hark! the ech-'ing air a tri - - - - - umph sings, a tri - - -

- - - - - - umph a tri - - - - - umph, tri - umph

sings _____   a tri - - - umph, tri - umph sings

And all__ a - round, and all__ a - round pleas'd_____ Cu-pids clap their wings, clap, clap,

clap,   clap their wings;   pleas'd_____ Cu - pids clap their wings;   and all__ a-

-round,   and all__ a - round,   pleas'd_____ Cu - pids clap, clap,

clap, clap, clap their wings, clap, clap, clap, clap, clap, clap, clap their wings, pleas'd

Cu-pids clap their wings And all __ a - wings.

Hark! hark! hark! hark! hark!
Hark! hark! hark! hark! hark!
Hark! hark! hark! hark! hark!
Hark! hark! hark! hark! hark!

HENRY PURCELL
Dido and Aeneas (1689), Act III, [scene 2]:

Dido: *Thy hand, Belinda—When I am laid in earth*

Extract of Purcell's *Dido and Aeneas* (edited by Margaret Laurie and Thurston Dart) reproduced from Purcell Society Edition Volume 3 by permission of Novello and Company Limited.

Chorus: *With drooping wings*

never, nev-er, nev - er part, and nev-er, nev-er, nev - er, nev - er part. With droop- part.

never, nev-er, nev - er part, and nev-er, nev-er, nev - er, nev - er part.   part.

nev-er, nev-er, nev - er part, and nev-er, nev-er, nev - er, nev - er part. With part.

nev-er, nev-er, nev - er part, and nev-er, nev-er, nev - er, nev - er part.   part.

Jean-Philippe Rameau (1683–1764)
Hippolyte et Aricie: Tragédie en 5 actes et un prologue (1733):
Act IV, Scene 1, *Ah! faut-il*

Rameau, *Oeuvres complètes*, VI, edited by Vincent d'Indy (Paris: Durand, 1900), pp. 262–67.

Ah! faut-il, en un jour, perdre tout ce que j'aime?

Et les maux que je crains, et les biens que je perds,

Tout accable mon coeur d'une douleur extrême.

Sous le nuage affreux dont mes jours sont couverts,

Que deviendra ma gloire aux yeux de l'univers?

Ah! faut-il, en un jour, perdre tout ce que j'aime?

Mon père pour jamais me bannit de ces lieux

Si chéris de Diane même.
Je ne verrai plus les beaux yeux
Qui faisaient mon bonheur suprême.

Ah, must I, in a day, lose all that I love?

And the troubles I fear, and the riches I lose,

all overwhelm my heart with extreme pain.

Under the terrible cloud that darkens my days,

what will become of my glory in the eyes of the world?
Ah, must I, in a day, lose all that I love?

My father is banishing me forever from these parts
so dear to Diane herself.
I shall see no more the beautiful eyes
which made me supremely happy.

SIMON–JOSEPH PELLEGRIN (1663–1745)

79

Alessandro Scarlatti (1660–1725)
Griselda (1721): Act II, Scene 1, Aria, *Mi rivedi, o selva ombrosa*

Reprinted by permission of the publishers from *The Operas of Alessandro Scarlatti,* Vol. III: *Griselda,* edited by Donald J. Grout and Elizabeth B. Hughes (Harvard Publications in Music, 8). Cambridge, Mass.: Harvard University Press, © 1975 by the President and Fellows of Harvard College.

più Re-gi-na e spo-sa, mi ri-ve-di sven-tu-ra-ta, di-sprez-za-ta pa-sto-rel- la.

Mi ri-ve-di o sel-va om-bro-sa, ma non più Re-gi-na e spo-sa, mi ri-

ve-di sven-tu-ra-ta, mi ri-ve-di sven-tu-ra- ta, di-sprez-za-ta, di-sprez-za-ta pa-sto-rel- la, sven-tu-

la no, non son più quel-la no, non son più, no, non son più quel - la _____. Mi ri-

Dal segno

GRISELDA

Mi rivedi o selva ombrosa,
Ma non più Regina e sposa,
Sventurata, disprezzata
Pastorella.
È pur quello il patrio monte,
Questa è pur l'amica fonte,
Quello è il prato e questo è il rio;
E sol io non son più quella.

You see me again, o shady forest,
but no longer queen and bride;
unfortunate, disdained,
a shepherdess.
Yet there is my homeland's mountain
and here is still the friendly fountain;
there is the meadow and this is the river;
and only I am not the same.

Based on the libretto by
APOSTOLO ZENO (1668–1750)

80

GEORGE FRIDERIC HANDEL (1685–1759)
Giulio Cesare: Act III, Scene 4 (excerpt)

Handel, *Werke,* edited by Friedrich Chrysander, Vol. 68 (Leipzig: Breitkopf und Härtel, 1875), pp. 102–8.

_ste er _ me a _ re_ne   al mo_nar_ca del mondo   er_rar con_vie_ne?   Au _ re,

au _ re, deh, per pie _ tà   spi _ ra _ te al pet _ to

mi _ o,   per dar con _ for_to,oh   Di _ o!   per dar con _ for_to,oh

Di_o!   al mio do _ lor,   al mio do_

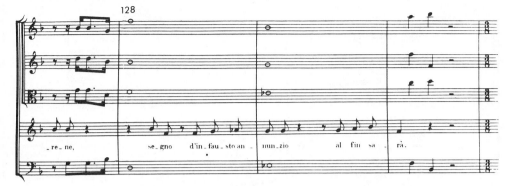

_re_ _ne,   se_ gno   d'in _ fau _ sto an _   nun _ zio   al fin sa _ rà.

Au _ re, deh, per pie _ tà   spi _ ra _ te al pet _ to   mi _ o,

per dar con _ for_to,oh   Di _ o   per dar   con _ for_to,oh   Di _ o

al mio do _ lor, _____   al mio   do _ lor,   al mio do_

CAESAR

Dall'ondoso periglio
Salvo mi porta al lido
Il mio propizio fato.
Quì la celeste parca
Non tronca ancor lo stame a la mia vita!
Mà dove andrò e chi mi porge aita?

Ove son le mie schiere?
Ove son le legioni,
Che a tante mie vittorie il varco apriro?
Solo in queste erme arene
Al monarca del mondo errar conviene?
Aure, aure, deh, per pietà
Spirate al petto mio,
Per dar conforto, oh Dio!
Al mio dolor.
Dite, dite dov'è
Che fà l'idolo del mio sen,
L'amato e dolce ben
Di questo cor.
Mà d'ogni intorno i' veggio
Sparse d'arme e d'estinti
L'infortuna arene,
Segno d'infausto annunzio al fin sarà.

From the perilous sea
safely takes me to the beach,
my propitious destiny.
Here heavenly fate
does not yet cut the thread of my life.
But where shall I go and who will come to my
    aid?
Where are my ranks?
Where are my legions,
that to so many victories opened the way?
In these solitary arenas
only the King of the World is at home.
Breezes, for pity's sake,
breathe on my breast
to comfort me, O God,
in my pain.
Tell me, where is she,
where is the idol of my heart,
beloved and sweet object
of this heart.
But all around me I see,
strewn with weapons and corpses,
this unfortunate arena,
an ill omen of my end.

NICOLA HAYM (1679–1729)

81

John Gay (1685–1732)*
The Beggar's Opera: Scenes 11 to 13

Scene XI

Mrs. Peach

The thing, husband, must and shall be done. For the sake of intelligence we must take other measures, and have him peach'd the next Session without her consent. If she will not know her duty, we know ours.

Peach

But really, my dear, it grieves one's heart to take off a great man. When I consider his personal bravery, his fine strategem, how much we have already got by him, and how much more we may get, methinks I can't find in my heart to have a hand in his death. I wish you could have made Polly undertake it.

Mrs. Peach

But in a case of necessity, our own lives are in danger.

Peach

Then, indeed, we must comply with the customs of the world, and make gratitude give way to interest. He shall be taken off.

Mrs. Peach

I'll undertake to manage Polly.

Peach

And I'll prepare matters for the Old-Baily.

Scene XII

Polly

Now I'm a wretch, indeed. Methinks I see him already in the cart, sweeter and more lovely than the nosegay in his hand! I hear the crowd extolling his resolution and intrepidity! What vollies of sighs are sent from the windows of Holborn, that so comely a youth should be brought to disgrace! I see him at the tree! The whole Circle are in tears! Even Butchers weep! Jack Ketch himself hesitates to perform his duty, and would be glad to lose his fee, by a reprieve. What then will become of Polly! As yet I may inform him of their design, and aid him in his escape. It shall be so. But then he

---

*Author of new texts set to existing songs. Gay's song texts are arranged in the left-hand column, the original texts and their sources in the right. Text and notes from *The Beggar's Opera by John Gay,* ed. Louis Kronenberger and Max Goberman (Larchmont: Argonaut Books, 1961), pp. xxxii–xxxiv.

flies, absents himself, and I bar myself from his dear dear conversation! That too will distract me. If he keep out of the way, my Papa and Mama may in time relent, and we may be happy. If he stays, stays, he is hang'd, and then he is lost for ever! He intended to lye conceal'd in my room, 'till the dusk of the evening: If they are abroad I'll this instant let him out, lest some accident should prevent him.

Exit, and returns

Scene XIII
Air XIV

Pretty Polly, say	Pretty Parret say,
When I was away,	When I was away,
Did your fancy never stray	And in dull absence pass'd the Day;
To some newer lover?	What at home was doing;
Without disguise,	With Chat and Play,
Heaving sighs,	We are Gay,
Doating eyes,	Night and Day,
My constant heart discover.	Good Chear and Mirth Renewing;
Fondly let me loll!	Singing, Laughing all,
[Fondly let me loll!]	Singing, Laughing all,
O pretty, pretty Poll.	Like pretty, pretty Poll.

PILLS TO PURGE MELANCHOLY—Vol. V

POLLY

And are you as fond as ever, my dear?

MACHEATH

Suspect my honour, my courage, suspect anything but my love. May my pistols miss fire, and my mare flip her shoulder while I am pursu'd, if I ever forsake thee!

POLLY

Nay, my dear, I have no reason to doubt you, for I find in the Romance you lent me, none of the great Heroes were ever false in love.

Air XV

MACHEATH

My heart was so free,	Come Fair one be kind,
It rov'd like the Bee,	You never shall find,
'Till Polly my passon requited;	A Fellow so fit for a Lover;
I sipt each flower,	The World shall view,
I chang'd every hour,	My Passion for you,
[I sipt each flower,	The World shall view,
I chang'd every hour,]	My Passion for you,
But here ev'ry flower is united.	But never your Passion discover.

PILLS TO PURGE MELANCHOLY—Vol. IV

POLLY

Were you sentenc'd to Transportation, sure, my dear, you could not leave me behind you—could you?

MACHEATH

Is there any power, any force that could tear me from thee? You might sooner tear a pension out of the hands of a Courtier, a fee from a Lawyer, a pretty woman from a looking–glass, or any woman from Quadrille. But to tear me from thee is impossible!

Air XVI

Were I laid on Greenland's coast,
And in my arms embrac'd my lass;
Warm amidst eternal frost,
Too soon the half year's night would pass.
Were I sold on Indian soil,
Soon as the burning day was clos'd,
I could mock the sultry toil,
When on my charmer's breast repos'd.
And I would love you all the day,
Every night would kiss and play,
If with me you'd fondly stray
Over the hills and far away.

Jockey was a bonny Lad,
And e'er was born in Scotland fair;
But now poor Jockey is run mad,
For Jenny causes his Despair;
Jockey was a Piper's Son,
And fell in Love while he was young:
But all the Tunes that he could play,
Was, o'er the Hills, and far away,
'Tis o'er the Hills, and far away,
'Tis o'er the Hills, and far away,
'Tis o'er the Hills, and far away,
The wind has blown my Plad away.

POLLY

Yes, I would go with thee. But oh! how shall I speak it? I must be torn from thee. We must part.

MACHEATH

How! Part!

POLLY

We must, we must. My Papa and Mama are set against thy life. They now, even now are in search after thee. They are preparing evidence against thee. Thy life depends upon a moment.

Air XVII

O what pain it is to part!
Can I leave thee, can I leave thee?
O what pain it is to part!
Can thy Polly ever leave thee?
But lest death my love should thwart,
And bring thee to the fatal cart,
Thus I fear thee from my bleeding heart!
Fly hence, and let me leave thee.

Gin thou wer't my e'ne Thing,
I wou'd Love thee I wou'd Love thee.
Gin thou wer't my e'ne Thing,
So Early I wou'd Love thee.
I wou'd take thee in my Arms,
I'de Secure thee From all Harms,
Above all Mortals thou has Charms,
So Dearly do I love thee.

ORPHEUS CALEDONIUS

POLLY

One kiss and then—one kiss—begone—farewell.

MACHEATH

My hand, my heart, my dear, is so riveted to thine, that I cannot unloose my hold.

POLLY

But my Papa may intercept thee, and then I should lose the very glimmering of hope. A few weeks, perhaps, may reconcile us all. Shall thy Polly hear from thee?

MACHEATH

Must I then go?

POLLY

And will not absence change your love?

MACHEATH

If you doubt it, let me stay—and be hang'd.

POLLY

O how I fear! How I tremble! Go. But when safety will give you leave, you will be sure to see me gain; for 'till then Polly is wretched.

Air XVIII

sight tis gone, Whines, whimpers, sobs and cries.

The Miser thus a shilling sees,
Which he's oblig'd to pay,
With sighs resigns it by degrees,
And fears 'tis gone for aye.
The Boy thus, when his Sparrow's flown,
The bird in silence eyes;
But soon as out of sight 'tis gone,
Whines, whimpers, sobs and cries.

O ye Broom, ye bonny, bonny Broom,
The Broom of Cowden-knows,
I wish I were at Home again
To milk my Daddys Ews.
How blyth ilk Morn was I to see
The Swain come o'er the Hill.
He skipt ye Burn and flew to me,
I met him with good Will.

82

George Frideric Handel

Serse

a) Act I, Scene 1, Recitativo accompagnato, *Frondi tenere;*
Aria *Ombra mai fù*

Reprinted by permission of Bärenreiter-Verlag, Kassel, Basel, Tours, London from: *Hallische Händel-Ausgabe,* edited by Rudolf Steglich (Kassel, 1958), pp. 9–11; 18–20.

b) Act I, Scene 3, Aria, *Và godendo vezzoso e bello*

go-den-do và _____ , vez-

zo-so e bel - lo   quel ru - scel-lo,   và go-den-do la li - ber-tà,   và   go-den-do   la li-ber-tà.

Adagio

a tempo

SERSE

Frondi tenere, e belle	Leaves, soft and lovely,
Del mio platano amato,	of my beloved plane-tree,
Per voi risplenda il Fato.	for you is Fate resplendent.
Tuoni, lampi, e procelle	Thunder, lightning, and gales
Non v'oltraggino mai la cara pace	never disturb your sweet peace;
Nè giunga a profanarvi astro rapace.	nor are you reached by the curse of an angry star.
Ombra mai fù di vegetabile	Never was there the shade of a plant
Cara ed amabile	more dear and lovable,
Soave più.	more sweet.

ROMILDA

Và godendo vezzoso e bello	Happily flowing, graceful and pretty,
Quel ruscello la libertà.	the brook enjoys its liberty.
E tra l'erbe con onde chiare	And among the grasses in clear ripples,
Lieto al mare correndo và.	merrily it goes running to the sea.

Based on the libretto by SILVIO
STAMPGILIA (1664–1725), which was
modeled on that by NICOLÒ MINATO (1654).

Giovanni Gabrieli (CA. 1553–1612)
Motet: *Hodie completi sunt dies pentecostes*
Antiphon at the Magnificat, Second Vespers,
Whitsunday

Gabrieli, *Symphoniae sacrae* (Venice, 1615). *Opera omnia,* edited by Denis Arnold, III (American Institute of Musicology) 1962), 44–56. Reprinted by permission of A. Carapetyan, Director and Hänssler-Verlag, West Germany. All rights reserved. International copyright secured.

55
-rit et bap-ti-za - tus, et bap-ti-za - tus fu-e - rit, sal - vus,
et bap-ti-za - tus, et bap-ti-za - tus fu - e-rit, sal - vus
et bap-ti-za - tus, et bap-ti-za - tus fu-e - rit, sal - vus
-rit et bap-ti-za - tus, et bap-ti-za - tus fu-e - rit. sal - vus,
-rit, et bap-ti-za - tus sal - vus, sal - vus, sal -
-rit et bap-ti-za - tus sal - vus, sal - vus,
-rit. et bap-ti-za - tus sal - vus, sal - vus, sal -
-rit, et bap-ti-za - tus sal - vus, sal - vus,
sal - vus, sal - vus, sal - vus, sal - vus e -
sal - vus, sal - vus, sal - vus e -
sal - vus, sal - vus, sal - vus, sal - vus
sal-vus, sal-vus, sal-vus, sal-vus
- vus, sal - vus, sal - vus, e - rit.
sal - vus, sal - vus e - rit.
- vus, sal - vus, sal - vus e - rit.
sal-vus, sal-vus, sal-vus e - rit.

Hodie completi sunt dies pentecostes, alleluia:
hodie Spiritus Sanctus in igne discipulis
apparuit et tribuit eis charismatum dona:
misit eos in universum mundum praedi-
care et testificari. Qui crediderit et bap-
tizatus fuerit, salvus erit, alleluia.

Today are ended the days of Pentecost, alleluia. Today the Holy Ghost appeared in
splendor to the disciples and bestowed
upon them the gifts of grace. He sent
them to preach and testify throughout the
world. He who believed was both baptized and saved. Alleluia.

84

Lodovico Grossi da Viadana (1560–1627)
Sacred Concerto: *O Domine Jesu Christe*

Reprinted by permission of Bärenreiter-Verlag, Kassel, Basel, Tours, London, from: *Cento concerti ecclesiastici opera duodecima* (Venice, 1602), edited by Claudio Gallico (Kassel, etc., 1964), pp. 64–65.

O Domine Jesu Christe,
pastor bone,
justos conserva
peccatores justifica,
omnibus fidelibus miserere,
et propitius esto mihi misero
et indigno peccatori. Amen.

O Lord Jesus Christ
good shepherd,
preserve the righteous,
do justice to the sinners,
have mercy on all the faithful,
and be gracious toward me, wretched
and unworthy sinner. Amen.

85

ALESSANDRO GRANDI (CA. 1575–1630)
Motet: *O quam tu pulchra es* (1625)

Values halved in triple meter. *Ghirlanda sacra, Libro primo . . . per Leonardo Simonetti* (Venice, 1625). Edited by Rudolf Werhart in *Drei Hohelied Motetten*, Cantio sacra, no. 23 (Cologne: Verlag Edmund Bieler, 1960), pp. 7–9. Reprinted by permission.

gre - ges ton - sa - - rum.   O ____ quam tu pul-chra   es.

Ve - ni,   ve - ni de   Li - ba-no,   ve - ni,   ve - ni de   Li - ba-no,

ve - ni, a - mi - ca me - a, co - lum - ba me - a, for - mo - sa me - a.

O ____ quam tu pul-chra es, ve - ni, ve - ni, co - ro - na - - be - ris.

Sur - ge,   sur - ge,   pro - pe - ra,   surge,   spon - sa   me - a,

surge, di - lec - ta me - a, surge, im - ma - cu - la - ta me - a.

surge, ve - ni, ve - ni, ve - ni, surge, ve - ni, ve - ni, ve - ni.

Qui - a a - mo - re lan - - - gue - o,

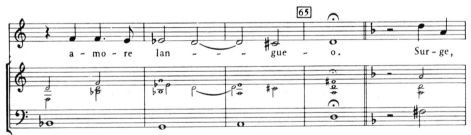

a - mo - re lan - - - gue - o. Sur - ge,

ve - ni, ve - ni, ve - - ni, sur - ge, ve - ni, ve - ni, ve - ni, qui -

a   a - mo - re,   a - mo - re lan - - gue - o.

O quam tu pulchra es, amica mea,
quam pulchra es, columba mea,
o quam tu pulchra es, formosa mea.
Oculi tui columbarum,
capilli tui sicut greges caprarum
et dentes tui sicut greges tonsarum.

O quam tu pulchra es.
Veni de Libano, amica mea,
columba mea, formosa mea.
O quam tu pulchra es,
veni, coronaberis.
Surge, surge, propera, sponsa mea,
surge, dilecta mea,
surge, immaculata mea.
Quia amore langueo.
Surge, veni, quia amore langueo.

Oh, how fair you are, my love,
how fair you are, my dove,
how fair you are, my beauty.
Your eyes, the eyes of doves,
your hair, like a flock of goats,
and your teeth like a flock of sheep newly
    shorn.
O how fair you are.
Come with me from Lebanon, my love,
my dove, my beauty.
Oh, how fair you are,
come, you will make a garland.
Arise, hasten, my bride,
arise, my delight,
arise, my spotless one.
For I pine of love. Arise,
come, for I pine of love.

            SONG OF SONGS, 4:1, 4:8

Giacomo Carissimi (1605–74)
Historia di Jephte

a) Filia, *Plorate, plorate colles*

Edited by Gottfried Wolters, figured bass realized by Mathias Siedel (Wolfenbüttel: Möseler Verlag, 1969), pp. 29–39. Reprinted by permission.

u - lu - -la - - - te, et in af-fli-cti - o - ne cor-dis me - i

u - lu - -la - - -te!

Eccho

u - - lu - -la - - te!

u - lu - la - - - te!

tasto solo

Ec - - ce mo - ri - ar vir - go et non pot - e - ro mor-te

me - a me - is fi - li - is con - so - la - - ri, in - ge - mi - sci - te

me do-len - tem   in lae-ti - ti-a po - pu-li,   in vi-cto - ri - a

Is - ra-el et glo-ri-a pa-tris me - i,   e - go si - ne

fi - li-is vir - - go, e - go fi-li-a u - ni - ge - ni-ta

mo - ri - ar et_____ non vi - - -

vam.   Ex-hor-re - sci - te ru - pes,   ob-stu-pe - sci - te col - les,

val - les et ca - ver - nae in so - ni - tu hor - ri - bi - li re - - - so -

na - te, val - les et ca - ver - nae in so - ni - tu hor - ri - bi - li, in

so - ni - tu hor - ri - bi - li re - - - - - so - na - te!

Plo - ra - te, plo -

Eccho

re - - - - so - na - te!

re - - - - so - na - te!

tasto solo

b) Chorus, *Plorate filii Israel*

DAUGHTER

Plorate colles, dolete montes
et in afflictione cordis mei
ululate! Ecce moriar virgo
et non potero morte mea meis
filiis consolari, ingemiscite
silvae, fontes et flumina, in in-
teritu virginis lachrimate,
fontes et flumina.

Heu me dolentem in laetitia
populi, in victoria Israel
et gloria patris mei, ego
sine filiis virgo, ego
filia unigenita moriar et
non vivam. Exhorrescite
rupes, obstupescite colles,
valles et cavernae in sonitu
horribili resonate!
Plorate, filii Israel,
plorate virginitatem meam et
Jephte filiam unigenitam in
carmine doloris lamentamini.

Plorate filii Israel, plorate
omnes virgines et filiam Jephte
unigenitam in carmine doloris
lamentamini.

Weep, hills, grieve, mountains
and in the affliction of my heart,
wail! Suddenly I shall die a
virgin and I shall not be able at my death
to be consoled by my children. Groan,
forests, springs, and rivers. Weep
for the death of a virgin,
springs and rivers.

Woe is me, sorrowful, amidst the joy
of the people in the victory of Israel
and the glory of my country, I,
without children, a virgin; I,
an only daughter, will die and
not live. Shudder,
crags; be stupefied, hills;
valleys and caves, resonate
the horrible sound.
Weep, sons of Israel,
bewail my virginity and lament
Jephte's only daughter in
songs of sorrow.

CHORUS

Weep, sons of Israel; weep,
all virgins, and lament Jephthe's
only daughter in songs of
sorrow.

87

HEINRICH SCHÜTZ (1585–1672)

Sacred concerto: *Saul, was verfolgst du mich*, SWV 415

Symphoniarum sacrarum tertia pars, worinnen zubefinden sind deutsche Concerten, op. 12 (Dresden, 1650), no. 18, ed. Günter Graulich and Paul Horn, Stuttgarter Schützausgabe (Stuttgart: Hänssler-Verlag, 1969), pp. 63–73.

65
mezzopiano
pianissimo
67
forte
mezzopiano
69
pianissimo
folgst du mich, was verfolgst du mich, was verfolgst du mich, was verfolgst du mich, was verfolgst du mich, was ver-
in-jure me, wilt thou in-jure me, wilt thou in-jure me, wilt thou in-jure me, wilt thou in-jure me, wilt thou
forte sempre
folgst du mich,
in-jure me,
Saul, Saul, Saul, Saul, Saul, Saul, Saul,
Saul, Saul, Saul, Saul, Saul, Saul, Saul,
was verfolgst du mich,
wilt thou in-jure me,

70
forte
mezzopiano
72
pianissimo
74
folgst du mich, was ver- folgst du mich, was ver- folgst du mich, was ver- folgst du mich,
in - jure me, wilt thou in - jure me, wilt thou in - jure me, wilt thou in - jure me,
Saul, Saul, Saul, Saul, was ver- folgst du mich,
Saul, Saul, Saul, Saul, wilt thou in - jure me,
solus
folgst du mich, was ver- folgst du mich, was ver- folgst du mich, was ver- folgst du mich, was ver- folgst du mich,
in - jure me, wilt thou in - jure me, wilt thou in - jure me, wilt thou in - jure me, wilt thou in - jure me,
was ver- folgst du mich,
wilt thou in - jure me,
Solo

88

Pelham Humfrey (1647–74)
Verse Anthem: *Hear O heav'ns*

Humfrey, *Complete Church Music,* edited by Peter Dennison (*Musica Britannica,* Vol. 34–35) (London: Published for the Royal Musical Association, 1972), pp. 82–89. Reproduced by permission of Stainer & Bell, Ltd. and the Musica Britannica Trust, London, England.

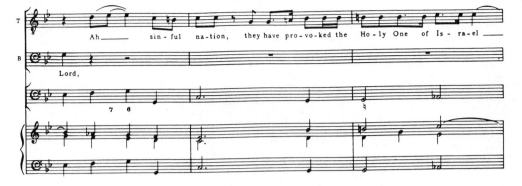

Ah ___ sin-ful na-tion, they have pro-vo-ked the Ho-ly One of Is - ra-el ___

Lord,

A

un - to an-ger, Ah ___ sin - ful, sin - ful

Ah ___ sin - ful na - tion, Ah sin - ful

seed of e - vil do - ers, child-ren that are cor-ru - pters, they have for - sa - ken the

na - tion,

na - tion,

89

George Frideric Handel

Oratorio: *Jephtha* (1752), Chorus, *How Dark, O Lord, are Thy decrees*

Text by Thomas Morell. Handel, *Werke, Ausgabe der deutschen Handelgesellschaft*, ed. Friedrich W. Chrysander (Leipzig, 1858–1903), 44:174–87.

turn _ ing,   and our   tri _ umphs   in _ to   mourn_ing,   as the   night   suc _ ceeds, suc _

_ sor _ row   turn _ ing,   and our   tri _ umphs   in _ to   mourn_ing,   as the   night   suc

_ceeds the   day,   all   our   joys   to_____   sor _ row

as the   night   suc _ ceeds the   day.

_ceeds the   day,   all   our   joys   to

as the   night   suc _ ceeds, suc _ ceeds   the   day,   suc _ ceeds   the   day,   as the

A tempo ordinario.

90

JOHANN SEBASTIAN BACH (1685–1750)
Cantata: *Nun komm, der Heiden Heiland*, BWV 61 (1714)

1a) Hymn, *Veni redemptor gentium*

Einsiedeln, Benediktinerkloster, Musikbibliothek, MS 366 (12th century), after Bruno Stäblein, ed., *Die mittelalterlichen Hymnenmelodien des Abendlandes, Monumenta monodica medii aevi*, Vol. I, Hymnen (I), pp. 273–74.

1b) Chorale, *Nun komm, der Heiden Heiland* BWV 61, Melody based on
Hymn, *Veni redemptor genitum*

Enchiridion Oder eyn Handbuchlein . . . geystlicher gesenge (Erfurt, 1524), after Johannes Zahn, *Die Melodien der deutschen evangelischen Kirchenlieder* (Gütersloh, 1892), Vol. I, No. 1174.

1c) Chorus, *Nun komm, der Heiden Heiland*

Music reprinted by permission of Bärenreiter-Verlag, Kassel, Basel, Tours, London from: *Neue Ausgabe sämtlicher Werke* Serie I, Band 1 edited by A. Dürr and W. Neumann. (Kassel, etc. 1954), pp. 3–16.

2) Recitative, *Der Heiland is gekommen*

3) Aria, *Komm, Jesu, komm zu deiner Kirche*

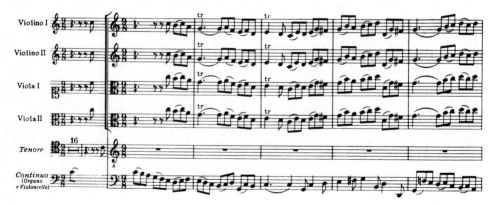

Be-för - dre dei - nes Na-mens Eh - re, er-hal-te

die_____ ge-sun-de Leh - re und seg-ne Kan-zel und_____ Al - tar!

Be-för-dre dei - nes Na-mens Eh - re, er-hal-te

die_____ ge-sun-de Leh - re und seg-ne Kan-zel und_____ Al - tar,   und seg-ne Kan - zel und Al -

tar,   und seg-ne Kan - zel und Al-tar,   und seg-ne Kan - zel und Altar!

Da Capo dal Segno 𝄌

4) Recitative, *Siehe, ich stehe vor der Tür*

Siehe, siehe, ich ste-he vor der Tür und klo-pfe an, und klopfe an. So je-mand mei-ne Stimme hö-ren wird

und die Tür auf-tun, zu dem werde ich ein-ge-hen und das Abendmahl mit ihm hal-ten, und er mit mir.

5) Aria, *Öffne dich, mein ganzes Herze*

6a) Chorale, *Wie schön leuchtet der Morgenstern*, Melody by Philipp Nicolai

Frewden Spiegel dess ewigen Lebens . . . durch Philippum Nicolai (Frankfurt, 1599), after Johannes Zahn, *Die Melodien der deutschen evangelischen Kirchenlieder* (Gütersloch, 1892), Vol. V, No. 8359.

6b) Chorus, *Amen. Komm du schöne Freudenkrone*

Hymn

Veni, redemptor gentium,
ostende partum virginis;
miretur omne saeculum,
talis decet partus deum.

Come, Savior of nations,
display the offspring of the Virgin.
Let all ages marvel
that God granted such a birth.

Chorale

Nun komm der Heiden Heiland
Der Jungfrauen Kind erkannt,
Des sich wundert alle Welt,
Gott solch Geburt ihm bestellt.

Now come, gentiles' Savior,
child, known to be born of the Virgin,
at which all the world marveled
that God such a birth for him ordained.

Recitative

Der Heiland ist gekommen,
Hat unser armes Fleisch und Blut
An sich genommen
Und nimmet uns zu Blutsverwandten an.
O allerhöchstes Gut,
Was hast du nicht an uns getan?
Was tust du nicht
Noch täglich an den Deinen?
Du kömmst und lässt dein Licht
Mit vollem Segen scheinen.

The Savior has arrived;
He has our poor flesh and blood
assumed,
and receives us as His blood-related kin.
O Supreme Good,
what have You not done for us?
What do You not
still daily do for Yours?
You come and leave Your light
with full blessings shining.

Aria

Komm, Jesu, komm zu deiner Kirche
Und gib ein selig neues Jahr!

Come, Jesus, come to your church,
and give a blessed new year!

Befördre deines Namens Ehre,   Advance Your name's honor,
Erhalte die gesunde Lehre   preserve the sane doctrine,
Und segne Kanzel und Altar!   and bless chancel and altar!

Recitative

"Siehe, ich stehe vor der Tür   "Behold, I stand at the door and
und klopfe an. So jemand meine   knock: if any man hear my
Stimme hören wird und die Tür   voice, and open the door,
auftun, zu dem werde ich eingehen   I will come into him
und das Abendmahl mit ihm halten   and will sup with him,
und er mit mir."   and he with me."

Aria

Öffne dich, mein ganzes Herze,   Open up, my whole heart,
Jesus kömmt und ziehet ein.   Jesus comes and takes possession.
Bin ich gleich nur Staub und Erde,   Though I am only dust and earth,
Will er mich doch nicht verschmähn,   Still He will not disdain
Seine Lust an mir zu sehn,   to show His delight
Dass ich seine Wohnung werde.   that I become His dwelling place.
O wie selig werd ich sein!   O how blessed will I be!

Chorale

Wie schön leuchtet der Morgenstern,   How fairly shines the morning star,
Voll Gnad und Wahrheit von dem Herrn,   full of grace and truth of the Lord,
Die füsse Wurzel Jesse!   the roots of the stock of Jesse.
Du Sohn Davids aus Jakobs Stamm,   You, son of David from Jacob's tribe,
Mein König und mein Bräutigam,   my king and my bridegroom,
Hast mir mein Herz besessen,   you have taken possession of my heart,
Lieblich, freundlich,   loving, friendly,
Schön und herrlich, gross und ehrlich,   handsome and magnificent, grand and honor-
                                                   able,
Reich von Gaben,   richly gifted,
Hoch und sehr prächtig erhaben.   tall and splendidly noble.

Chorale

Amen,   Amen,
Amen.   Amen.
Komm du schöne Freudenkrone, und bleib   Come, you beautiful crown of joy; and tarry
   nicht lange.   not.
Deiner wart' ich mit Verlangen.   I wait for you with longing.

91

JOHANN SEBASTIAN BACH
"Mass in B Minor," BWV 232,
Symbolum Nicenum (Credo)

a) *Et in Spiritum sanctum Dominum*

The title "Mass in B minor" was added after the composer's time. It is questionable whether the compilation constitutes a Mass or whether it can be said to be in B minor. (a) *Et in Spiritum;* and (b) *Confiteor* date from 1747–49; (c) *et expecto* is based on the Chorus, "Jauchzet, ihr erfreuten Stimmen" (second movement) of Cantata BWV 120, *Gott, man lobet dich in der Stille,* for the inauguration of the new town-council (*Rathswechsel*) in 1728 or 1729. Reprinted by permission of Bärenreiter-Verlag Kassel, Basel, Tours, London from: *Neue Ausgabe sämtlicher Werke,* edited by Friedrich Smend. (Kassel, etc. 1954), pp. 190–215.

et in Spi-ri-tum san-ctum Do - mi-num et vi - vi - fi - can - tem, vi - vi-fi-

can - tem, Spi-ri-tum san-ctum, Spi-ri-tum san-ctum vi-vi-fi - can-tem, vi - vi-fi - can-tem Do - mi-

num, qui ex Pa - tre Fi - li - o - - - - que pro-ce - - - - - - -

- - - - dit, ex Pa - tre Fi - li-o-que pro-ce - dit, qui ex Pa - - tre Fi - li - o - -

- - que pro-ce - - dit;

phe-tas lo-cu-tus est,   lo-cu-tus est per Pro-phe - - - tas,   lo-cu-tus est per Pro-

phe - - - tas, per Pro-phe - tas.   Et u-nam san-ctam ca-tho-li-cam et a-pos-to-li-

cam ec-cle - - - si-am,

et u-nam san-ctam ca-tho-li-cam et a-pos-to-li-

cam ec-cle-si-am,   et u-nam san-ctam   ca-tho - - - - - - -

b) *Confiteor*

c) *Et expecto resurrectionem*

85
li, ven - tu - ri se - cu - li, a - men, a -
li, ven - tu - ri se - cu - li, a - men, a -
li, ven - tu - ri se - cu - li, a - men, a - men,
li, ven - tu - ri se - cu - li, a - men, a - men, a - men,
li, ven - tu - ri se - cu - li, a - men,

For a translation of the text see p. 16.

92

Giovanni Legrenzi (1626–90)
Trio Sonata, *La Raspona*

Sonate a due, e tre di Giovanni Legrenzi, Libro primo, Opera seconda (Venice, 1655). Reprinted by permission of Bärenreiter-Verlag, Kassel, Basel, Tours, London, from *Hortus Musicus,* No. 31, edited by Werner Danckert (Kassel, 1949), pp. 3–7.

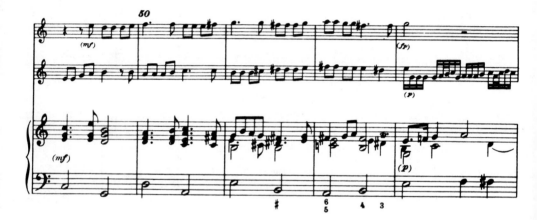

93

Arcangelo Corelli (1653–1713)
Trio Sonata, Op. 3, No. 2

From *Sonate a tre* (Bologna, 1689). *Les Oeuvres de Arcangelo Corelli,* edited by J. Joachim and F. Chrysander (London, n.d.), pp. 130–35.

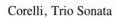

Allegro.

Allegro.

94

GIUSEPPE TORELLI (1658–1709)
Concerto for Violin, Op. 8, No. 8, Allegro
(last movement)

Concerti grossi con una pastorale per il Santissimo Natale (Bologna, 1709).

95

ANTONIO VIVALDI (1678–1741)
Concerto grosso in G minor, Op. 3, No. 2

a) Adagio e spiccato (first movement)

Vivaldi, *L'Estro armonico*, Op. 3 (Amsterdam, 1712). Edited by Gian Francesco Malipiero (Milan: Ricordi, 1965), Vol. 407, pp. 1–33; F. IV, no. 8; Pincherle 326. Reprinted by permission.

10

b) Allegro (second movement)

20

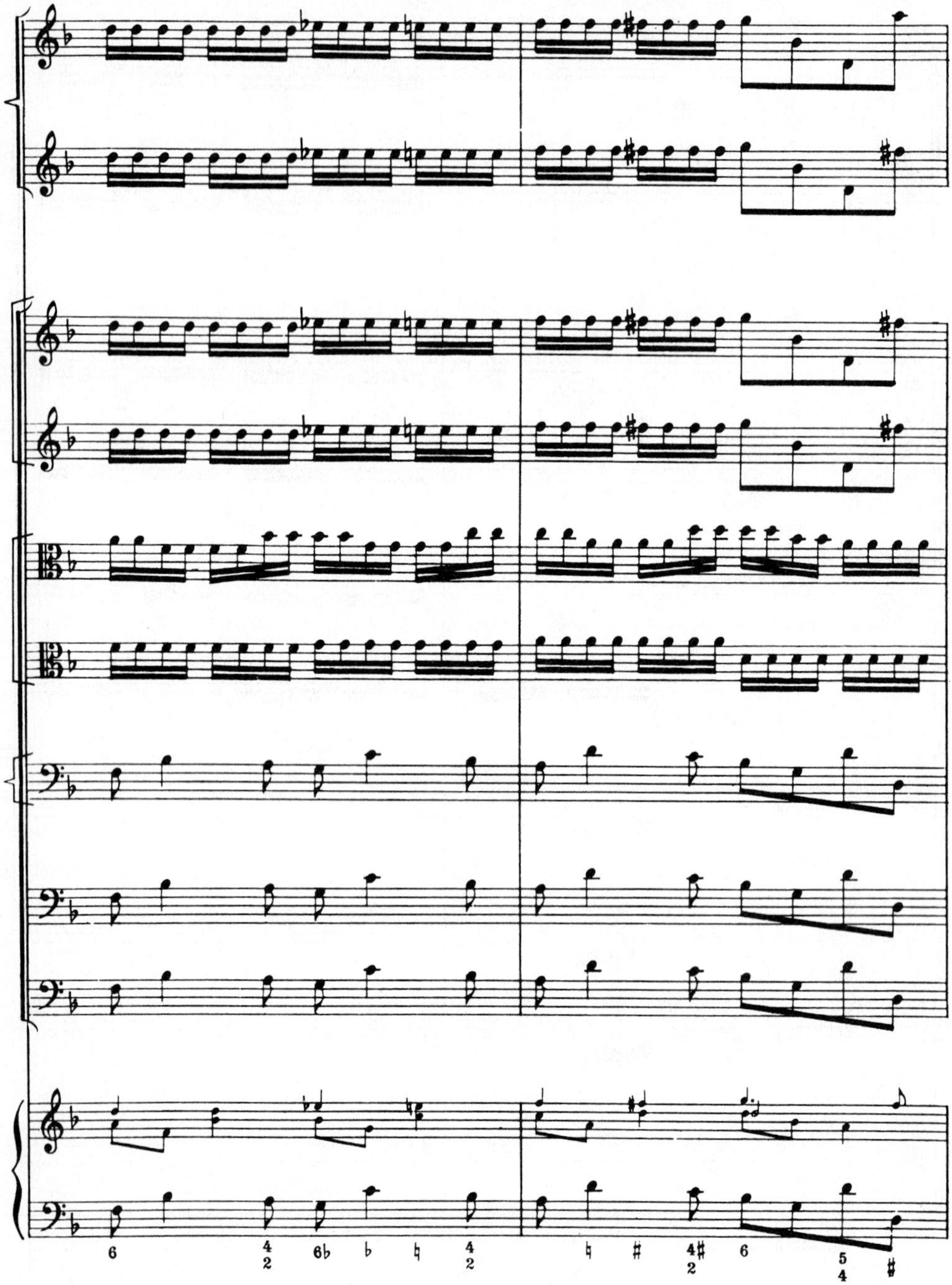
6
4
2
6♭
♭
♮
4
2
♮
♯
4♯
2
6
5
4
♯

30

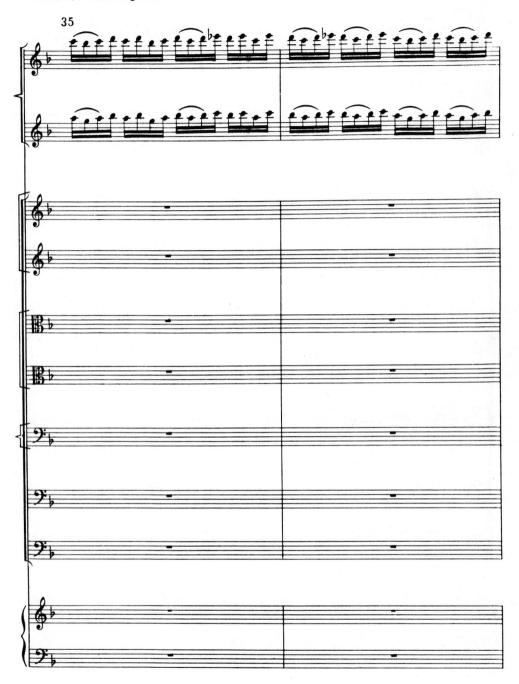

Antonio Vivaldi
Concerto for Violin, Op. 9, No. 2: Largo (second movement)

Vivaldi, *La Cetra* (Amsterdam, 1728). Edited by Gian Francesco Malipiero (Milan: Ricordi, 1952), Vol. 126, pp. 18–19; F. I, 51; Pincherle 214. Reprinted by permission.

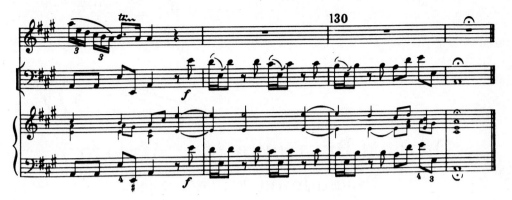

97

Dietrich Buxtehude (ca. 1637–1707)
Praeludium, buxwv 141

Dietrich Buxtehude, *Sämtliche Orgelwerke,* ed. Josef Hedar, 2:79–84 (Copenhagen: Wilhelm Hansen Nr. 3922).

DIETRICH BUXTEHUDE
Chorale Prelude: *Danket dem Herrn denn er ist sehr freundlich,* BUXWV 181

Dietrich Buxtehudes Werke für Orgel, ed. Phillip Spitta, *Neue Ausgabe* von Max Seiffert, II (Leipzig, 1904), 1–2. Reprinted by permission of Breitkopf & Härtel, Wiesbaden.

[Versus 3] tertio modo

JOHANN SEBASTIAN BACH
Durch Adams Fall, BWV 637

a) Chorale melody

Durch A-dams Fall ist ganz ver-derbt Mensch-lich Na-tur und We - sen;
Das - selb Gift ist auf uns ge-erbt, Dass wir nicht moch-ten g'ne - sen

Ohn Got - tes Trost, der uns er - löst Hat von dem gros-sen Scha - den

Dar - ein die Schlang' Hie - nam be-zwang, Gotts Zorn auf sich zu la - den.

a) Text by Lazarus Spengler. *Geistliche Lieder auffs new gebossert* (Wittemberg: Joseph King, 1535), after Johannes Zahn, *Die Melodien der deutschen evangelischen Kirchenlieder* (Gütersloh, 1892), Vol. IV, No. 7549.

Durch Adams Fall ist ganz verderbt	Through Adam's fall is entirely spoiled
Menschlich Natur und Wesen;	both human nature and character.
Dasselb Gift ist auf uns geerbt,	The same venom was by us inherited,
Dass wir nicht mochten g'nesen	so that we could not recover from it
Ohn Gottes Trost,	without God's solace,
Der uns erlöst	that saves us
Hat von dem grossen Schaden,	from great harm;
Darein die Schlang	for the serpent
Hienam bezwang,	somehow managed
Gotts Zorn auf sich zu laden.	to take onto itself God's anger.

LAZARUS SPENGLER

b) Organ chorale

This is one of the chorales Bach entered into the *Orgelbüchlein* (Little Organ Book), which he began to compile in Weimar (1716–17) and continued in Köthen (1717–23) but never finished.

100

Johann Sebastian Bach
Chorale Preludes, *Wenn wir in höchsten Noten sein* (two settings)

a) Chorale melody

The text, by Paul Eber (1511–69), was set to this melody by Franz Eler in *Cantica sacra* (Hamburg, 1588). The melody was composed by Louis Bourgeois (*ca.* 1515–after 1561) to the French hymn, "Leve le coeur, ouvre l'oreille," published in *Psaulmes cinquante de David . . . traduictz en vers françois par Clément Marot* (Lyons, 1547).

Wenn wir in höchsten Nöten sein	When we are in greatest need
Und wissen nicht, wo aus noch ein,	and know not which way to go,
Und finden weder Hilf noch Rat,	and find neither help nor counsel,
Ob wir gleich sorgen früh und spat,	whether our worries come early or late,
So ist dies unser Trost allein,	then this alone is our comfort,
Dass wir zusammen insgemein,	that we together as one
Dich anrufen, o treuer Gott,	call upon you, o true God,
Um Rettung aus der Angst und Not.	for rescue from our anguish and misery.

b) Organ Chorale, BWV 641

From the *Orgelbüchlein* (see No. 99). Reprinted by permission of Bärenreiter-Verlag, Kassel, Basel, Tours, London from *Neue Ausgabe sämtliche Werke*, Serie IV, Oregel Werke, Band 2, edited by Hans Klotz (Kassel, 1972), pp. 212–14.

c) Organ Chorale, BWV 668a

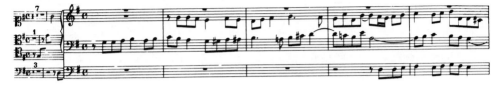

Edited by Hans Klotz from a Leipzig-period dictated copy (1750?) in *Neue Ausgabe sämtlicher Werke*, Serie IV, *Orgelwerke*, Band 2, pp. 212–14 (Kassel: Bärenreiter-Verlag, 1958); see the facsimile in *ibid.*, p. xiii. Reprinted by permission.

Johann Sebastian Bach
Praeludium et Fuga, BWV 543

Reprinted by permission of Bärenreiter-Verlag Kassel, Basel, Tours, London from: *Neue Ausgabe sämtliche Werke*, Serie IV, Orgel Werke, Band 5. edited by Dietrich Kilian (Kassel, 1972), pp. 186–97.

Variations on Dowland's *Lachrimae Pavan*

a) John Dowland, *Lachrimae Pavana*

The Collected Lute Music of John Dowland, transcribed and edited by Diana Poulton and Basil Lam (London: Faber; Kassel: Bärenreiter-Verlag, 1974), pp. 67–70. Reprinted by permission.

b) William Byrd, *Pavana Lachrymae*

The Fitzwilliam Virginal Book, edited by J. A. Fuller Maitland and W. Barclay Squire (Leipzig: Breitkopf & Härtel, 1899), II, 42–46.

Jan Pieterszoon Sweelinck
Fantasia a 4

Opera omnia, Vol. I: *The Instrumental Works,* edited by Gustav Leonhardt, Alfons Annegarn, and Frits Noske (Amsterdam: Vereniging voor Nederlandse Muziekgeschiedenis, 1968), pp. 26–34. Used by permission.

Girolamo Frescobaldi (1583–1643)
Toccata No. 3 (1637)

Toccata Terza

Toccate d'intavolatura di cimbalo et organo libro 1 (Rome, 1637; first published in *Il primo libro d'intavolatura di toccate di cimbalo et organo,* 1628), ed. Pierre Pidoux, Orgel- und Klavierwerke 3 (Kassel: Bärenreiter, 1954):11–13.

105

ENNEMOND GAUTIER (CA. 1575–1651)
Gigue: *La Poste* for Lute

a) Gautier: arrangement for lute

Special signs: *pincé* (mordent with lower auxiliary); *coulé* (upward double appoggiatura); *port de voix* (appoggiatura starting on lower auxiliary) *Oeuvres du vieux Gautier,* edited by André Souris (Paris: Éditions du CNRS, 1966), Nos. 63, 85, pp. 83, 111.

b) Anonymous arrangement for harpsichord

FRANÇOIS COUPERIN (1668–1733)
Vingt-cinquième ordre (1730) (excerpts)

a) *La Visionaire*

For a guide to the realization of Couperin's ornaments, see *HWM*, 4th ed., p. 456. *Pièces de Clavecin, 4ième Livre*, edited by Kenneth Gilbert © 1970 Heugel et Cie. Reprinted by permission. Theodore Presser Company, sole Representative U.S.A.

b) *La Misterieuse*

c) *La Monflambert*

Tendrement, sans lenteur

d) *La Muse victorieuse*

Audacieusement

e) *Les Ombres errantes*

Languissamment

Appendix A
Instrument Names and Abbreviations

The following tables set forth the English, Italian, German, and French names used for the various musical instruments in these scores, and their respective abbreviations.

WOODWINDS

English	Italian	German	French
Piccolo (Picc.)	Flauto piccolo (Fl. Picc.)	Kleine Flöte (Kl. Fl.)	Petite flûte
Flute (Fl.)	Flauto (Fl.); Flauto grande (Fl. gr.)	Grosse Flöte (Fl. gr.)	Flûte (Fl.)
Alto flute	Flauto contralto (fl.c-alto)	Altflöte	Flûte en sol
Oboe (Ob.)	Oboe (Ob.)	Hoboe (Hb.); Oboe (Ob.)	Hautbois (Hb.)
English horn (E. H.)	Corno inglese (C. or Cor. ingl., C.i.)	Englisches Horn	Cor anglais (C. A.)
Sopranino clarinet	Clarinetto piccolo (clar. picc.)		
Clarinet (C., Cl., Clt., Clar.)	Clarinetto (Cl. Clar.)	Klarinette (Kl.)	Clarinette (Cl.)
Bass clarinet (B. Cl.)	Clarinetto basso (Cl. b., Cl. basso, Clar. basso)	Bass Klarinette (Bkl.)	Clarinette basse (Cl. bs.)
Bassoon (Bsn., Bssn.)	Fagotto (Fag., Fg.)	Fagott (Fag., Fg.)	Basson (Bssn.)
Contrabassoon (C. Bsn.)	Contrafagotto (Cfg., C. Fag., Cont. F.)	Kontrafagott (Kfg.)	Contrebasson (C. bssn.)

BRASS

English	Italian	German	French
French horn (Hr., Hn.)	Corno (Cor., C.)	Horn (Hr.) [pl. Hörner (Hrn.)]	Cor; Cor à pistons
Trumpet (Tpt., Trpt., Trp., Tr.)	Tromba (Tr.)	Trompete (Tr., Trp.)	Trompette (Tr.)
Trumpet in D	Tromba piccola (Tr. picc.)		

English	Italian	German	French
Cornet	Cornetta	Kornett	Cornet à pistons (C. à p., Pist.)
Trombone (Tr., Tbe., Trb., Trm., Trbe.)	Trombone [pl. Tromboni (Tbni., Trni.)]	Posaune.(Ps., Pos.)	Trombone (Tr.)
Tuba (Tb.)	Tuba (Tb, Tbaı)	Tuba (Tb.)	Tuba (Tb.)

PERCUSSION

English	Italian	German	French
Percussion (Perc.)	Percussione	Schlagzeug (Schlag.)	Batterie (Batt.)
Kettledrums (K. D.)	Timpani (Timp., Tp.)	Pauken (Pk.)	Timbales (Timb.)
Snare drum (S. D.)	Tamburo piccolo (Tamb. picc.) Tamburo militare (Tamb. milit.)	Kleine Trommel (Kl. Tr.)	Caisse claire (C. cl.), Caisse roulante Tambour militaire (Tamb. milit.)
Bass drum (B. drum)	Gran cassa (Gr. Cassa, Gr. C., G. C.)	Grosse Trommel (Gr. Tr.)	Grosse caisse (Gr. c.)
Cymbals (Cym., Cymb.)	Piatti (P., Ptti., Piat.)	Becken (Beck.)	Cymbales (Cym.)
Tam-Tam (Tam-T.)			
Tambourine (Tamb.)	Tamburino (Tamb.)	Schellentrommel, Tamburin	Tambour de Basque (T. de B., Tamb. de Basque)
Triangle (Trgl., Tri.)	Triangolo (Trgl.)	Triangel	Triangle (Triang.)
Glockenspiel (Glocken.)	Campanelli (Cmp.)	Glockenspiel	Carillon
Bells (Chimes)	Campane (Cmp.)	Glocken	Cloches
Antique Cymbals	Crotali Piatti antichi	Antiken Zimbeln	Cymbales antiques
Sleigh Bells	Sonagli (Son.)	Schellen	Grelots
Xylophone (Xyl.)	Xilofono	Xylophon	Xylophone

STRINGS

English	Italian	German	French
Violin (V., Vl., Vln, Vi.)	Violino (V., Vl., Vln.)	Violine (V., Vl., Vln.) Geige (Gg.)	Violon (V., Vl., Vln.)
Viola (Va., Vl., *pl.* Vas.)	Viola (Va., Vla.) *pl.* Viole (Vle.)	Bratsche (Br.)	Alto (A.)
Violoncello, Cello (Vcl., Vc.)	Violoncello (Vc., Vlc., Vcllo.)	Violoncelì (Vc., Vlc.)	Violoncelle (Vc.)
Double bass (D. Bs.)	Contrabasso (Cb., C. B.) *pl.* Contrabassi or Bassi (C. Bassi, Bi.)	Kontrabass (Kb.)	Contrabasse (C. B.)

OTHER INSTRUMENTS

English	Italian	German	French
Harp (Hp., Hrp.)	Arpa (A., Arp.)	Harfe (Hrf.)	Harpe (Hp.)
Piano	Pianoforte (P.-f., Pft.)	Klavier	Piano
Celesta (Cel.)			
Harpsichord	Cembalo	Cembalo	Clavecin
Harmonium (Harmon.)			
Organ (Org.)	Organo	Orgel	Orgue
Guitar		Gitarre (Git.)	
Mandoline (Mand.)			

Appendix B
Glossary

a. The phrases *a 2, a 3* (etc.) indicate that the part is to be played in unison by 2, 3 (etc.) players; when a simple number (1., 2., etc.) is placed over a part, it indicates that only the first (second, etc.) player in that group should play.

abdämpfen. To mute.

aber. But.

accelerando (acc.). Growing faster.

accompagnato (accomp.). In a continuo part, this indicates that the chord-playing instrument resumes (*cf. tasto solo*).

adagio. Slow, leisurely.

a demi-jeu. Half-organ; i.e., softer registration.

ad libitum (ad lib.). An indication giving the performer liberty to: (1) vary from strict tempo; (2) include or omit the part of some voice or instrument; (3) include a cadenza of his own invention.

agitato. Agitated, excited.

alla breve. A time signature (₵) indicating, in the sixteenth century, a single breve per two-beat measure; in later music, the half note rather than the quarter is the unit of beat.

allargando (allarg.). Growing broader.

alle, alles. All, every, each.

allegretto. A moderately fast tempo (between allegro and andante).

allegro. A rapid tempo (between allegretto and presto).

alto, altus (A.). The deeper of the two main divisions of women's (or boys') voices.

am Frosch. At the heel (of a bow).

am Griffbrett. Play near, or above, the fingerboard of a string instrument.

amoroso. Loving, amorous.

am Steg. On the bridge (of a string instrument).

ancora. Again.

andante. A moderately slow tempo (between adagio and allegretto).

animato,animé. Animated.

a piacere. The execution of the passage is left to the performer's discretion.

arco. Played with the bow.

arpeggiando, arpeggiato (arpeg.). Played in harp style, i.e. the notes of the chord played in quick succession rather than simultaneously.

assai. Very.

a tempo. At the (basic) tempo.

attacca. Begin what follows without pausing.

auf dem. On the (as in *auf dem G,* on the G string).

Auftritt. Scene.

Ausdruck. Expression.

ausdrucksvoll. With expression.

Auszug. Arrangement.

baguettes. Drumsticks (*baguettes de bois, baguettes timbales de bois,* wooden drumsticks or kettledrum sticks; *baguettes d'éponge,* sponge-headed drumsticks; *baguettes midures,* semi-hard drumsticks; *baguettes dures,* hard drumsticks; *baguettes timbales en feutre,* felt-headed kettledrum sticks).

bariton. Brass instrument.

bass, basso, bassus (B.). The lowest male voice.

Begleitung. Accompaniment.

belebt. Animated.

beruhigen. To calm, to quiet.

bewegt. Agitated.

bewegter. More agitated.

bien. Very.

breit. Broadly.

breiter. More broadly.

Bühne. Stage.

cadenza. An extended passage for solo instrument in free, improvisatory style.

calando. Diminishing in volume and speed.

cambiare. To change.

cantabile (cant.). In a singing style.

cantando. In a singing manner.

canto. Voice (as in *col canto,* a direction for the accompaniment to follow the solo part in tempo and expression)

cantus. An older designation for the highest part in a vocal work.

chiuso. Stopped, in horn playing.

col, colla, coll'. With the.

come prima, come sopra. As at first; as previously.

comme. Like, as.

comodo. Comfortable, easy.

con. With.

Continuo (Con.). A method of indicating an accompanying part by the bass notes only, together with figures designating the chords to be played above them. In general practice, the chords are played on a lute, harpsichord or organ, while, often, a viola da gamba or cello doubles the bass notes.

contratenor. In earlier music, the name given to the third voice part which was added to the basic two voice texture of discant and tenor, having the same range as the tenor which it frequently crosses.

corda. String; for example, *seconda (2a) corda* is the second string (the A string on the violin).

coro. Chorus.

coryphée. Leader of a ballet or chorus.

countertenor. Male alto, derived from *contratenor altus.*

crescendo (cresc.). Increasing in volume.

da capo (D.C.). Repeat from the beginning, usually up to the indication *Fine* (end).

daher. From there.

dal segno. Repeat from the sign.

Dämpfer (Dpf.). Mute.

decrescendo (decresc., decr.). Decreasing in volume.

delicato. Delicate, soft.

dessus. Treble.

détaché. With a broad, vigorous bow stroke, each note bowed singly.

deutlich. Distinctly.

diminuendo, diminuer (dim., dimin.). Decreasing in volume.

discantus. Improvised counterpoint to an existing melody.

divisés, divisi (div.). Divided; indicates that the instrumental group should be divided into two or more parts to play the passage in question.

dolce. Sweet and soft.

dolcemente. Sweetly.

dolcissimo (dolciss.). Very sweet.

Doppelgriff. Double stop.

doppelt. Twice.

doppio movimento. Twice as fast.

doux. Sweet.

drängend. Pressing on.

e. And.

Echoton. Like an echo.

éclatant. Sparkling, brilliant.

einleiten. To lead into.

Encore. Again.

en dehors. Emphasized.

en fusée. Dissolving in.

erschütterung. A violent shaking, deep emotion.

espressione intensa. Intense expression.

espressivo (espress., espr.). Expressive.

et. And

etwas. Somewhat, rather.

expressif (express.). Expressive.

falsetto. Male singing voice in which notes above the ordinary range are obtained artificially.

falsobordone. Four-part harmonization of psalm tones with mainly root-position chords.

fauxbourdon (faulx bourdon). Three-part harmony in which the chant melody in the treble is accompanied by two lower voices, one in parallel sixths, and the other improvised a fourth below the melody.

fermer bresquement. To close abruptly.

fine. End, close.

flatterzunge, flutter-tongue. A special tonguing technique for wind instruments, producing a rapid trill-like sound.

flüchtig. Fleeting, transient.

fois. Time (as in *premier fois*, first time).

forte (f). Loud.

fortissimo (ff). Very loud (*fff* indicates a still louder dynamic).

fortsetzend. Continuing.

forza. Force.

frei. Free.

fugato. A section of a composition fugally treated.

funebre. Funereal, mournful.

fuoco. Fire, spirit.

furioso. Furious.

ganz. Entirely, altogether.

gebrochen. Broken.

gedehnt. Held back.

gemächlich. Comfortable.

Generalpause (G.P.). Rest for the complete orchestra.

geschlagen. Struck.

geschwinder. More rapid, swift.

gesprochen. Spoken.

gesteigert. Intensified.

gestopft (chiuso). Stopped; for the notes of a horn obtained by placing the hand in the bell.

gestrichen (gestr.). Bowed.

gesungen. Sung.

geteilt (get.). Divided; indicates that the instrumental group should be divided into two parts to play the passage in question.

gewöhnlich (gew., gewöhnl.). Usual, customary.

giusto. Moderate.

gleichmässig. Equal, symmetrical.

gli altri. The others.

glissando (gliss.). Rapidly gliding over strings or keys, producing a scale run.

grande. Large, great.

grave. Slow, solemn; deep, low.

gravement. Gravely, solemnly.

grazioso. Graceful.

grossem. Large, big.

H⌐ Hauptstimme, the most important voice in the texture.

Halbe. Half.

Halt. Stop, hold.

harmonic (harm.). A flute-like sound produced on a string instrument by lightly touching the string with the finger instead of pressing it down.

Hauptzeitmass. Original tempo.

heftiger. More passionate, violent.

hervortretend. Prominently.

Holz. Woodwinds.

hörbar. Audible.

immer. Always.

impetuoso. Impetuous, violent.

istesso tempo. The same tempo, as when the duration of the beat remains unaltered despite meter change.

klagend. Lamenting.

klangvoll. Sonorous, full-sounding.

klingen lassen. Allow to sound.

kräftig. Strong, forceful.

kurz. Short.

kurzer. Shorter.

laissez vibrer. Let vibrate; an indication to the player of a harp, cymbal, etc., that the sound must not be damped.

langsam. Slow.

langsamer. Slower.

largamente. Broadly.

larghetto. Slightly faster than largo.

largo. A very slow tempo.

lebhaft. Lively.

legato. Performed without any perceptible interruption between notes.

leggéro, leggiero (legg.). Light and graceful.

legno. The wood of the bow (*col legno tratto*, bowed with the wood; *col legno battuto*, tapped with the wood; *col legno gestrich*, played with the wood).

leidenschaftlich. Passionate, vehement.

lent. Slow.

lentamente. Slowly.

lento. A slow tempo (between andante and largo).

l.h. Abbreviation for "left hand."

lié. Tied.

ma. But.

maestoso. Majestic.

maggiore. Major key.

main. Hand (*droite*, right; *gauche*, left).

marcatissimo (marcatiss.). With very marked emphasis.

marcato (marc.). Marked, with emphasis.

marcia. March.

marqué. Marked, with emphasis.

mässig. Moderate.

mean. Middle part of a polyphonic composition.

meno. Less.

mezza voce. With half the voice power.

mezzo forte (mf). Moderately loud.

mezzo piano (mp). Moderately soft.

minore. In the minor mode.

minuetto. Minuet.

mit. With

M. M. Metronome; followed by an indication of the setting for the correct tempo.

moderato, modéré. At a moderate tempo.

molto. Very, much.

mosso. Rapid.

motetus. In medieval polyphonic music, a voice part above the tenor; generally, the first additional part to be composed.

moto. Motion.

muta, mutano. Change the tuning of the instrument as specified.

N̄ Nebenstimme, the second most important voice in the texture.

Nachslag. Auxiliary note (at end of trill).

nehmen (nimmt). To take.

neue. New.

nicht, non. Not.

noch. Still, yet.

octava (okt., 8va). Octave; if not otherwise qualified, means the notes marked should be played an octave higher than written.

ohne (o.). Without.

open. In brass instruments, the opposite of muted. In string instruments, refers to the unstopped string (i.e. sounding at its full length).

ordinario, ordinairement (ordin., ord.). In the usual way (generally cancelling an instruction to play using some special technique).

ôtez les sourdines. Remove the mutes.

parlando. A singing style with the voice approximating speech.

parte. Part (*colla parte*, the accompaniment is to follow the soloist in tempo).

passione. Passion.

pause. Rest.

pedal (ped., P.). In piano music, indicates that the damper pedal should be depressed; an asterisk indicates the point of release (brackets below the music are also used to indicate pedalling). On an organ, the pedals are a keyboard played with the feet.

perdendosi. Gradually dying away.

peu. Little, a little.

pianissimo (pp). Very soft (*ppp* indicates a still softer dynamic).

piano (p). Soft.

più. More.

pizzicato (pizz.). The string plucked with the finger.

plötzlich. Suddenly, immediately.

plus. More.

pochissimo (pochiss.). Very little.

poco. Little, a little.

poco a poco. Little by little.

ponticello (pont.). The bridge (of a string instrument).

portato. Performance manner between legato and staccato.

prenez. Take up.

près de la table. On the harp, the plucking of the strings near the soundboard.

prestissimo. Very fast.

presto. A very quick tempo (faster than allegro).

prima. First.

principale (pr.). Principal, solo.

quasi. Almost, as if.

quasi niente. Almost nothing, i.e. as softly as possible.

quintus. An older designation for the fifth part in a vocal work.

rallentando (rall., rallent.). Growing slower.

rasch. Quick.

recitative (recit.). A vocal style designed to imitate and emphasize the natural inflections of speech.

rinforzando (rinf.). Sudden accent on a single note or chord.

ritardando (rit., ritard.). Gradually slackening in speed.

ritmico. Rhythmical.

rubato. A certain elasticity and flexibility of tempo, speeding up and slowing down, according to the requirements of the music.

ruhig. Calm.

ruhiger. More calmly.

saltando (salt.). An indication to the string player to bounce the bow off the string by playing with short, quick bow-strokes.

sans. Without.

scherzando (scherz.). Playfully.

schleppend. Dragging.

schnell. Fast.

schneller. Faster.

schon. Already.

schwerer. Heavier, more difficult.

schwermütig. Dejected, sad.

sec., secco. Dry, simple.

segno. Sign in form of :S: indicating the beginning and end of a section to be repeated.

segue. (1) Continue to the next movement without pausing; (2) continue in the same manner.

sehr. Very.

semplice. Simple, in a simple manner.

sempre. Always, continually.

senza. Without.

senza mis[ura]. Free of regular meter.

serpent. Bass of the cornett family.

seulement. Only.

sforzando, sforzato (sfz, sf). With sudden emphasis.

simile. In a similar manner.

sino al . . . Up to the . . . (usually followed by a new tempo marking, or by a dotted line indicating a terminal point).

sombre. Dark, somber.

son. Sound.

sonore. Sonorous, with full tone.

sopra. Above; in piano music, used to indicate that one hand must pass above the other.

soprano (Sop., S.) The voice with the highest range.

sordino (sord.). Mute.

sostenendo, sostenuto (sost.). Sustained.

sotto voce. In an undertone, subdued, under the breath.

sourdine. Mute.

soutenu. Sustained.

spiccato. With a light bouncing motion of the bow.

spirito. Spirited, lively.

spiritoso. In a spirited manner.

sprechstimme (sprechst.). Speaking voice.

staccato (stacc.). Detached, separated, abruptly disconnected.

stentando, stentato (stent.). Delaying, retarding.

Stimme. Voice.

strepitoso, strepito. Noisy, boisterous.

stretto. In a non-fugal composition, indicates a concluding section at an increased speed.

stringendo (string.). Quickening.

subito (sub.). Suddenly, immediately.

sul. On the (as in *sul G*, on the G string).

suono. Sound, tone.

superius. The uppermost part.

sur. On.

Takt. Bar, beat.

tasto solo. In a continuo part, this indicates that only the string instrument plays; the chord-playing instrument is silent.

tempo primo (tempo I). At the original tempo.

tendrement. Tenderly.

tenerezza. Tenderness.

tenor, tenore (T., ten.). High male voice or part.

tenuto (ten.). Held, sustained.

touche. Fingerboard or fret (of a string instrument).

tranquillo. Quiet, calm.

trauernd. Mournfully.

treble. Soprano voice or range.

tremolo (trem). On string instruments, a quick reiteration of the same tone, produced by a rapid up-and-down movement of the bow; also a rapid alteration between two different notes.

très. Very.

trill (tr.). The rapid alternation of a given note with the note above it. In a drum part it indicates rapid alternating strokes with two drumsticks.

triplum. In medieval polyphonic music, a voice part above the tenor.

tristement. Sadly.

troppo. Too much.

tutti. Literally, "all"; usually means all the instruments in a given category as distinct from a solo part.

übertönend. Drowning out.

unison (unis.). The same notes or melody played by several instruments at the same pitch. Often used to emphasize that a phrase is not to be divided among several players.

Unterbrechung. Interruption, suspension.

veloce. Fast.

verhalten. Restrained, held back.

verklingen lassen. To let die away.

Verwandlung. Change of scene.

verzweiflungsvoll. Full of despair.

vibrato. Slight fluctuation of pitch around a sustained tone.

vif. Lively.

vigoroso. Vigorous, strong.

vivace. Quick, lively.

voce. Voice.

volti. Turn over (the page).

Vorhang auf. Curtain up.

Vorhang fällt, Vorhang zu. Curtain down.

voriges. Preceding.

vorwärts. Forward, onward.

weg. Away, beyond.

wieder. Again.

wie oben. As above, as before.

zart. Tenderly, delicately.

ziemlich. Suitable, fit.

zurückhaltend. Slackening in speed.

zurückkehrend zum. Return to, go back to.

Index of Composers

Index of Titles

Index of Forms and Genres

Index to NAWM References in *A History of Western Music*, 4th Ed.